E-Marketing

Steve Shipside

MARKETING 04.03

- *The* fast track route to mastering all aspects of e-marketing

- Covers all the key techniques for successful e-marketing, from affiliate marketing to e-mail alerts, and from viral marketing to banner ads

- Examples and lessons from some of the world's most successful businesses, including Hotmail, Pepsi and Honda, and ideas from the smartest thinkers, including Christopher Locke and Seth Godin

- Includes a glossary of key concepts and a comprehensive resources guide

essential management thinking at your fingertips

The right of Steve Shipside to be identified as the author of this work has been asserted in accordance with the Copyright, Designs and Patents Act 1988

First published 2002 by
Capstone Publishing (A Wiley Company)
8 Newtec Place
Magdalen Road
Oxford OX4 1RE
United Kingdom
http://www.capstoneideas.com

CIP catalogue records for this book are available from the British Library and the US Library of Congress

ISBN 1-84112-199-1

This book is printed on acid-free paper

Substantial discounts on bulk quantities of Capstone books are available to corporations, professional associations and other organizations. Please contact Capstone for more details on +44 (0)1865 798 623 or (fax) +44 (0)1865 240 941 or (e-mail) info@wiley-capstone.co.uk

Contents

Introduction to ExpressExec

ExpressExec is 3 million words of the latest management thinking compiled into 10 modules. Each module contains 10 individual titles forming a comprehensive resource of current business practice written by leading practitioners in their field. From brand management to balanced scorecard, ExpressExec enables you to grasp the key concepts behind each subject and implement the theory immediately. Each of the 100 titles is available in print and electronic formats.

Through the ExpressExec.com Website you will discover that you can access the complete resource in a number of ways:

» printed books or e-books;
» e-content – PDF or XML (for licensed syndication) adding value to an intranet or Internet site;
» a corporate e-learning/knowledge management solution providing a cost-effective platform for developing skills and sharing knowledge within an organization;
» bespoke delivery – tailored solutions to solve your need.

Why not visit www.expressexec.com and register for free key management briefings, a monthly newsletter and interactive skills checklists. Share your ideas about ExpressExec and your thoughts about business today.

Please contact elound@wiley-capstone.co.uk for more information.

Introduction to E-Marketing

This chapter briefly covers:

» the phenomenal rise and extent of e-marketing;
» its place in worldwide commerce today;
» pointers to the future; and
» its nature as a more intimate medium than may be supposed from its reach.

"People of Earth ... A powerful global conversation has begun.
Through the Internet, people are discovering and inventing new
ways to share relevant knowledge with blinding speed. As a
direct result, markets are getting smarter – and getting smarter
faster than most companies. These markets are conversations.
Their members communicate in language that is natural, open,
honest, direct, funny, and often shocking. Whether explaining or
complaining, joking or serious, the human voice is unmistakably
genuine. It can't be faked."

So begins the *ClueTrain Manifesto*, the so-called "end of business as
usual" and one of the most widely discussed contributions to the subject
of e-marketing. Part business theory, part copywriter's handbook, part
"beat poet meets PR," the manifesto touches on many points but all
relate to its one central tenet: "Markets are conversations."

Which is the whole point of e-marketing. Don't be misled by that
"e." E-marketing is not about technologies, e-marketing is simply about
voices, about talking and about listening. As with so much that purports
to be simple there is a catch, a monumental hiccup in the proceeding
of events and one succinctly expressed by the author of *Permission
Marketing*, Seth Godin:

"YOU'RE NOT PAYING ATTENTION. NOBODY IS."
"It's not your fault. It's just physically impossible for you to pay
attention to everything that marketers expect you to – like the
17,000 new grocery store products that were introduced last year,
or the $1,000 worth of advertising that was directed exclusively at
you last year."

Wherein lies the rub. The technologies are there for mass communication on a scale never before imagined. There have never been so
many means of messaging; not just the Web, or traditional e-mail, but
faxback services, interactive television, SMS (short messaging service)
text messages to phones, paging, and the forthcoming broadband third
generation (3G) phones featuring animation and video. Previously mute
devices are developing voices. In-car computers and wristwatch pagers
are with us now, Web-ready domestic appliances are on their way. The

number of devices that can communicate is huge. More importantly, unlike mass media of the past, the new generation of communication devices is increasingly personal; part and parcel of our lives, with the accompanying promise that a good marketer can establish ever more intimate links with individuals.

The problem is that everyone wants our attention, and getting yourself heard has never been harder. Bad marketing is nothing but noise, another contribution to the swelling hubbub that means most of us aren't paying attention. The guaranteed route to bad e-marketing is to look at the astonishing reach of modern media, and see that as a way of making more noise, only louder and more intrusively. Good e-marketing sees that the way to cut through that hullabaloo is not by shouting, but by talking, conversing, engaging people in a two-way flow of interactive information.

What the hardcore adherents of e-marketing will tell you is that e-marketing isn't just another addition to the marketing mix, another tool in the box. Instead they point out that the way people communicate is permanently changing the way that markets work. Diversification of media makes it harder to make a point simply by shouting so loudly that you drown out other people's messages. On the Web your rivals, and indeed your dissatisfied customers, are only a click away.

Instead, successful marketers are retaining attention less by talking, and more by listening. They are not just dumb devices that are being given the power of speech. Individuals now have voices that can span continents. WWW might just as well stand for World Wide Word of mouth.

The manifesto-writing messiahs of new media pronounce that this is "the end of business as usual" and of the traditional relationship to markets. Whether or not you go along with the revolutionary zeal, there is no doubt that for the e-marketer this is the beginning of a whole new chapter.

What is E-Marketing?

In answering this question, the writings of leading experts are considered in:

» defining the nature of e-marketing media;
» noting differences from mass media;
» demonstrating the growth of direct marketing;
» recognizing a new breed – the e-customer cometh; and
» key insights.

On one level, e-marketing is simply the use of electronic channels of communication to spread your marketing messages. New media including the Web, mobile phones, and interactive TV can all be harnessed as part of the marketing mix.

That's one view of e-marketing. The other is that trying to put the Web into the same toolbox as broadcasting and print is to miss the point completely. The way that the Web works is totally unlike any other medium, and part and parcel of that is a totally new dynamic between the marketer and his or her audience. Here is a somewhat aquatic way of looking at it:

> "If your delivery medium was water, broadcasting would be like using a big hose to spray a crowd of prospects, hoping some of them will enjoy getting wet. Narrowcasting, a term used by producers of specialized cable TV programs, is like using a smaller hose and only aiming it at people who have already expressed an interest in getting wet. Cybercasting (marketing online) is the act of creating a pond of water in cyberspace, telling people that you now have a pond, and inviting them to come for a swim. Prospects can visit your pond anytime they want, stay as long as they want, and dive in as deeply as they want. The extent to which they immerse themselves in your pond is determined completely by their own personal interest."
>
> *Kristin Zhivago, publisher of the Marketing Technology*
> *newsletter (www.zhivago.com).*

The combination of the World Wide Web and personal information devices offers an extraordinary blend of wide reach and personal targeting. That, plus the ease of consumer response, makes e-marketing an opportunity to turn conventional marketing wisdom on its head and in the process establish an entirely new relationship with consumers and markets. Unfortunately not all marketers are glad to be told that they are going to have to re-think everything they know, as the following extract points out:

> "Marketers have gotten comfortable with the methods they've been using for the past four decades. Market share. Segmentation.

CPMs, GRPs, ratings and shares. Psychographic and geodemographic analysis. These have become the shrines of a religion to the mass marketer. Some say the game is changing. Wrong. The game is over, and when we all wake up (tomorrow morning) in the dawn of the Information Age, the mass marketers will be holding their aching heads, trying to figure out what happened to their credentials.

"Nearly a hundred years ago, mass production made mass marketing possible. But it was the rise of mass media, in the form of radio and national magazines, that mandated mass marketing. Likewise, new developments in technology make mass customized production possible, but it is the fractionalization of mass media and the rise of one-to-one (1:1) media that mandate 1:1 marketing. "The heart of 1:1 marketing will be a focus on winning a greater share of each customer's business precisely because marketers now have the computational power to remember every detail about a customer's transaction history, and that includes communication."

Don Peppers and Martha Rogers from One-to-One Media in the Interactive Future (published in Cybermarketing, NTC Business Books, 1997).

That one-to-one approach shouldn't intimidate marketers. It is after all the goal of direct marketing, but with the twist that in e-commerce there is the possibility of reverse direct marketing – of the consumer reaching out for the message. Direct marketing is growing at a remarkable rate, but it is wrong to see the Web as simply another means of direct mail, minus the postage costs. At its best, direct marketing on the Web is like normal direct marketing on steroids. A leading guru of the new media foresees its greatly enhanced effectiveness in the context of a new, yet familiar discipline, which he calls "permission marketing":

"Marketers now allocate about 52% of their annual ad budgets for direct mail and promotions, a significant increase over past years. A 2% response for a direct mail campaign will earn the smart marketer a raise at most companies. But a 2% response means that the same campaign was trashed, ignored or rejected by an amazing 98% of the target audience! From the perspective of the marketer, however, if the campaign earns more than it costs, it's worth doing again.

"Imagine your marketing message being read by 70% of the prospects you send it to (not 5% or even 1%). Then imagine that more than 35% respond. That's what happens when you interact with your prospects one at a time, with individual messages, exchanged with their permission over time. Permission marketing is anticipated, personal, relevant. Anticipated – people look forward to hearing from you. Personal – the messages are directly related to the individual. Relevant – the marketing is about something the prospect is interested in.

"Permission marketing has been around forever (or at least as long as dating!), but it takes advantage of new technology better than other forms of marketing. The Internet is the greatest direct mail medium of all time, and the low cost of frequent interaction makes it ideal for permission marketing..."

Seth Godin, Permission Marketing (Simon & Schuster).

The problem is that this proactive consumer, the e-customer, who is expected to give permission and then anticipate marketing messages, is not the simple customer of yesterday:

"The e-customer is an enhanced, magnified version of everything that homo consumer has always wanted to be."

Max Mckeown, E-Customer: Inspire the Wired Generation.

It's not that *homo sapiens* has changed; rather that *homo consumer* is now empowered to a remarkable degree, with the ability to consult other consumers in their hundreds of thousands, and send messages back to the marketers. The idea of the e-customer is therefore both exhilarating and terrifying to traditional marketing which has had the luxury of being able to treat consumers as a mute and malleable mass audience. Mckeown also wrote an article called "The Mind of the E-Customer" which is really an open letter to e-marketers everywhere:

"You don't know me. I'm the e-customer. You talk like you know me. Invested as though you understood what I really want. The government paid for the first twenty years of the Internet. Investors paid for the next 10 years. Who is left? I am the only one that will pick up the tab for your future e-commerce plans. So open up your heart and hear this. There is no joy to be found in doing a half a job for me and there's very little money either. You need to get into my mind."

Max Mckeown, The Mind of the E-Customer.

Marketing has never been more resistible than when it is on the Web. The Net itself was designed to be able to carry on and reroute traffic even around potential war damage. If consumers perceive advertising as damage they too will reroute around it. Where a single click can close windows and transport users to another site it becomes very hard for an e-marketer to stop someone for long enough to listen to a message from their sponsor. It's a challenge, but not an impossible one. Seth Godin offers a different slant on a basic marketing necessity – the idea:

"We live in a world where consumers actively resist marketing. So it's imperative to stop marketing at people. The idea is to create an environment where consumers will market to each other. Is an idea virus a form of marketing? Sure it is. And today, marketing is all there is. You don't win with better shipping or manufacturing or accounts payable. You win with better marketing, because marketing is about spreading ideas, and ideas are all you've got left to compete with."

Seth Godin, Unleashing the Idea Virus.

Nor should it be forgotten that e-marketing is not a honed art, or a long-established science, but a very new branch of marketing indeed. Dating back only about half a decade it is literally being made up as we go along, and progress is not as smooth as some would have you believe. As futurist John Naisbitt (www.naisbitt.com) observes:

"The gee-whiz futurists are always wrong because they believe technological innovation travels in a straight line. It doesn't. It weaves and bobs and lurches and sputters."

Megatrends, Warner Books 1982.

In e-marketing those sputters are already evident; think of all the fuss behind "push" media trying to broadcast to the Web, or the ups and downs of the banner ad. E-marketing is enabled by technology, but it most certainly is not about computers, browsers, programming languages or bandwidth. More than anything else e-marketing is about a new attitude to the audience, and a new role for that audience. When the conditions are right, the market becomes the e-marketer.

KEY INSIGHTS

» The greatest shift in e-marketing is not technological; it is about the relationship between marketer and market.

» The Web provides the greatest-ever means for direct marketing.

» E-marketing is still in its infancy, and has some more stumbling to do before it can learn to walk.

The Evolution of E-Marketing

A resumé of the new discipline, including:

» history of the Net;
» beginning of the Web;
» early signs of commercialization;
» the explosion of online advertising;
» beyond the banner; and
» timeline.

ORIGINS OF A REVOLUTION

Whilst the broader definition of electronic marketing includes devices such as the fax, and the interactive computer kiosk, the term e-marketing is primarily used about the potential of the Internet, and technologies such as wireless communications and interactive TV which are often expected to hook up with the Net to provide both information and communications channels. As such, the evolution of e-marketing is really a series of disparate threads drawn together, including the creation of the Internet, the development of the World Wide Web, and a shift in marketing thinking from mass media towards personalization; from the desire to target demographic groups to the need to single out individual consumers.

On the technical side e-marketing owes its origins to some spectacularly unlikely people – on the one hand the US Department of Defense, and on the other a group of European scientists so serious-minded that the creator of the Web itself, Tim Berners-Lee, didn't originally intend it to have such fripperies as pictures.

You could say that every e-marketer today owes a debt of thanks to Vladimir Ilyich Lenin. Or at least to the Union of Soviet Socialist Republics he helped to found. The USSR's rivalry with the West, and the subsequent 'cold war', was the reason why the US Defense Advanced Research Projects Agency (DARPA to its friends) commissioned a company called BBN to create a network of computers called the ARPANET in 1969. The story goes that the final decision was triggered by the news that the Russians had put a sputnik into orbit and the US was afraid of losing the technological upper hand. The idea of the new computer network was that it would be able not only to send messages around the country, but to do so even if certain parts of the country were to be suddenly vaporized in the event of nuclear war.

The system worked by linking up all the existing government computers, forming a network of networks, which meant that there were many different routes for information to take. It also required the development of an addressing system to identify computers on the system, and individuals demanding information, and a way of splitting up data, sending it, and then checking that it was all there at the other end.

This idea of interlinked computers had applications well beyond military needs, and scientific and educational establishments were keen to connect to each other via the system. In 1988 the first commercial e-mail system, MCI, was given permission to use it, and the keystone was laid for the e-mail marketing schemes of today.

THE WEB IS BORN ...

That was the Net. The Web on the other hand, the publishing arena that sits on the framework of the Net, owes its existence to a British scientist called Tim Berners-Lee and his work at CERN, the European physics laboratory. In the 1980s Berners-Lee, in an effort to make sense of its massive information system, used hyperlinks to allow users to jump from one related document to another, and a layout language that could display the results. To see all this he invented a new piece of software, the browser – albeit a very no-frills form from a modern perspective – which he made publicly available in 1990. The Web was born, although it was a far cry from the commercial behemoth we know today.

... AND GOES COMMERCIAL

Marketing too was going through some pronounced changes. The mass markets and mass media that had evolved in the first half of the twentieth century had brought with them the idea of mass advertising. Direct marketing, always a hit-and-miss approach at best, received a distinct boost from the advent of computers able to compile databases and perceive patterns. By the 1980s the PC was with us, and with it computing came within the reach of any marketing company.

By the end of the decade an idea was coming into vogue that would shift marketing dramatically away from the "any color you want, as long as it's black" mentality established by Henry Ford. "Relationship marketing" worked on the basis that even the economy of scale offered by mass marketing left plenty of scope for carving out market niches by tailoring products to a specific group of customers. Regis McKenna published the seminal work *Relationship Marketing* in 1991, stressing that good marketing needed to involve dialogue with the customer base and a willingness to reshape the product depending on feedback.

In 1993 Don Peppers and Martha Rogers took that a step further with the book *The One-to-One Future*. Peppers and Rogers argued that customer acquisition was so much more expensive than customer retention that the job of marketing would shift more towards learning about existing customers. "In the one-to-one future," they noted, "it won't be how much you know about all of your customers that's important, but how much you know about each of your customers." To do that you needed better two-way dialogue, and although the Web's commercial potential was still a pipedream the pair discussed the possibility of electronic communications to do this.

ADVERTISING – THE NEXT LEAP FORWARD

Before 1993 the Web was still perceived both from inside and outside as the last place you'd want to place an advertisement. The more serious academic communities (and presumably the military) weren't in a rush to see the Web plastered with advertisements, and initially the public and commercial perception of the Web was that it was some kind of wild frontier, an anarchic and lawless place unfit for the marketing of family brands. That didn't last. By 1993 advertisements were appearing on Websites, and the first banner ad (the Web's equivalent of the poster ad format) popped up sometime in 1994 on the pages of hotwired.com, the bible of the new medium. That year also saw the very first online shopping malls appear as traditional retailers and their upstart rivals alike saw the potential for e-commerce. A deeply relieved population of couch potatoes and latenight surfers was finally able to order Pizza Hut pizza without having to loosen their grasp on the mouse.

By 1995 Poppe Tyson had spun off its young ad sales unit to form DoubleClick, and the concepts of tracking, both in terms of traffic numbers and exactly how people behaved on a site, were well established. In the UK a small multimedia company called NoHo Digital produced a screensaver for Ogilvy & Mather. It featured a thirsty Guinness drinker jigging around the screen while waiting for his pint of Guinness to be poured. The screensaver, the pint, and the dancer were soon to be bobbing around on computer screens all over the country after a word of mouth campaign that resulted in it being known as *that* screensaver. Viral multimedia marketing was now part of the UK media landscape even if the phrase still meant little or nothing to most marketers.

By 1997 Peppers and Rogers popped up again with *The One-to-One Enterprise*, which argued that it was necessary not only to have dialogue with customers, but to do it on a huge scale, at low cost, and with the ability to track and report fully on online campaigns. By now there were a few more marketers ready to take the message onboard, not least because the message was spreading about the reach of online campaigns, and the degree to which they could be accurately reported in terms of page impressions, individual users, and click-through patters. The formation of the Internet Advertising Bureau (IAB) in 1996 added credence to the Web as a marketing medium, and the inauguration of the quarterly Advertising Revenue Report, conducted independently for the IAB by the New Media Group of PricewaterhouseCoopers, gave advertising skeptics a handle on the development of the new medium.

The figures were impressive. Quarter on quarter growth suggested that online advertising was muscling its way into the traditional media landscape. By the end of 1998 the IAB was able to report that Internet advertising revenues had exceeded $1.92bn, thereby easily surpassing the estimated $1.58bn in revenue garnered by outdoor advertising. The 1998 online advertising revenue grew by 112% over the $906.5mn for 1997. Fourth quarter 1998 revenues increased $165mn (34%) over the same quarter for 1997, to $655.6mn, establishing it as the twelfth consecutive record-setting quarter for the industry.

IAB chairman Rich LeFurgy was talking for the whole industry when he declared that "it is easy for us to forget that the Internet, as a viable advertising medium, is barely four years old, and it is astounding, that in such a relatively short period of time, its growth is now measured in billions of dollars. It is significant to note that Internet advertising has not reached a plateau, and we expect that with online ad budgets increasing for current advertisers, and the growing number of large traditional advertisers who are migrating their advertising to the Internet, we look forward to a sustained period of growth in the years ahead."

That growth and those figures meant that advertising agencies could no longer afford to denigrate the upstart medium, and the once independent multimedia agencies were quickly being snapped up to form the core of a new wave of Interactive Marketing Departments at the heart of the established agencies. Stories emerged from across the industry that there remained a major cultural gap between these new interactive divisions and their new parent companies; in particular it was felt that the Net was being treated as a broadcast medium – an extremely slow speed television. By 2000 however two major factors were starting to force a rethink of the nature of online marketing. The first was that the great dotcom boom was on the wane; the second was that the marketing landscape was fragmenting, and the banner advertisement format – previously the mainstay of any campaign – was starting to lose prominence.

NEW FASHIONS, NEW FORMATS

In 2000 the dotcom boom had yet to turn into the full-fledged "dotgone" crash, but the turndown was affecting the amount of easy money previously sloshing around in marketing budgets. At the end of the third quarter of 2000 the IAB reports showed an increase of 63% over the comparative quarter for 1999, but showed a slight decline of 6.5% when compared with the second quarter of 2000. That still translated to an annual revenue of over $8bn.

Tom Hyland, chairman of the PricewaterhouseCoopers New Media Group observed that "Because of the robust nature of this medium, we have become accustomed to continued, unfettered growth." Despite the slowdown, however, Hyland also pointed out that this did not mean that the medium had peaked: "We believe that it is important to note that in a comparatively weaker advertising market, Internet ad revenues still totaled nearly $2bn for the quarter. This is still the fastest growing medium ever, subject to the vagaries of the marketplace, but still recognized by advertisers, both small and large, as the place they have to be to insure success."

"This slight decline in online ad revenue should come as no surprise to the industry" concluded Rich LeFurgy, chairman of the IAB. LeFurgy attributed the slowdown to "the pull-back of advertising by many companies in the dotcom sector, combined with the traditionally weak third quarter, and the transition of the advertisers' focus on how to best take advantage of the Internet."

This last comment is the most telling for the e-marketer. If traditional advertising had been slow to come to terms with the Net, it could at least understand the banner format which functioned in much the same way as advertisements in other media. However, as Websites multiplied, the banner ad, with its traditional goal of driving site traffic, was having a hard time. In response, marketers were turning to a whole raft of alternative ways of getting their message across. "With publishers offering a variety of new and innovative ad formats these advertisers are now transitioning their objectives," observed LeFurgy. "Increasingly aware of the power of the medium for branding and direct marketing, these savvy advertisers are no longer looking for the most traffic; rather, they are seeking different ways and new creative formats which publishers are offering to build their brands. This is an industry of innovation, and the serious players are in it for the long haul."

From almost total domination of the ad picture, by the end of 2000 banner ads accounted for only 46%, with the remainder being made up by sponsorships (28%), classifieds (9%), referrals (6%), interstitials (4%), e-mail (2%), rich media (2%), keyword searches (2%), and other (2%). By the following year the revenue share of banner ads was down to 40%, sponsorships and classifieds had both risen by 3%, and e-mail had doubled to 4%. With click-through rates on banners down to under a third of 1% the impetus to find new ways to communicate is growing. Or as Robin Webster, the current president and CEO of the IAB puts it: " I believe that all interactive media have the ability to react quicker and with more creativity than more traditional advertising platforms, and can offer advertisers compelling new formats and channels to reach consumers. I am confident that we will continue to see the growing emergence of new ad formats and the integration of overall campaigns, with the Internet becoming an increasingly important part of the media buy."

TIMELINE

» **1969**
  » Arpanet is commissioned
» **1988**
  » MCI, the first commercial e-mail service, is given permission to use the Net

» **1990**
  » Tim Berners-Lee publishes the first browser and the Web is born
» **1991**
  » Regis McKenna publishes *Relationship Marketing*
» **1993**
  » Peppers and Rogers publish *The One-to-One Future*
» **1994**
  » Shopping malls appear on the Net
  » Pizza from Pizza Hut can now be ordered online
  » The first banner ads appear on hotwired.com in October – for Zima (a drink) and AT&T
» **1995**
  » DoubleClick is spun off from Poppe Tyson
  » Guinness screensaver storms the small screen in the UK
» **1996**
  » Conducted by the New Media Group of PricewaterhouseCoopers on an ongoing basis, with results released quarterly, the "Advertising Revenue Report" is started by the IAB (Internet Advertising Bureau)
  » Total Internet ad spending reaches $267mn according to the IAB
» **1997**
  » $906.5mn is spent on online advertising (IAB)
  » Peppers and Rogers publish *The One-to-One Enterprise*
» **1998**
  » May 4, the two millionth domain name (voyagerstravel.com) is registered
  » For the first time, Internet advertising revenue exceeds one billion dollars within the same calendar year, totaling $1.3bn through the nine months ending September 1998 (IAB)
» **1999**
  » The *ClueTrain* Manifesto is posted on the Web
  » March 9, the four millionth domain name (riedelglass.com) is registered
  » May 29, the five millionth domain name (believeinkids.com) is registered
  » Global ad spending online reaches $4.3bn (according to Jupiter)

» **2000**
  » The ten millionth domain name is registered
  » Web size (estimated by the pages indexed by search engine Inktomi) goes beyond the one billion page mark
  » Global ad spending online reaches $8.2bn (IAB)
» **2001**
  » Global ad spending online reaches $10.4bn (Jupiter)
» **2005**
  » Global ad spending online reaches $27.7bn (Jupiter)

KEY INSIGHTS

» E-marketing came about by accident, not design.
» The technology that makes it possible was created for the military, exploited by scientists and academia, and only now is the third, commercial phase in full swing.
» Never has a medium grown so significantly. It took radio some 40 years to reach a 50 million audience. TV took just under 15, Cable TV took ten, and the Net took less than five.

Because of that it has been misunderstood in many ways, first as a publishing medium, then as a broadcast medium, and only now is its full impact as an interactive medium starting to show.
» While the Net is unlikely to show ever again the triple figure percentage growth of the early years of advertising, it is still growing into a significant medium for the advertising industry. For all the ups and downs, slowdowns and booms, the e-marketer is catching up on his more established peers.

The E-Dimension

The challenge of the Internet:

- » not another mass medium;
- » the hunt for eyeballs;
- » measuring: hits, clickthroughs and impressions;
- » decline of the banner;
- » from interruption to influencers; and
- » good practice case study.

AN INTIMATE MEDIUM

The most crucial factor of e-marketing is not the fact that it can reach millions instantly or that it can do so for near zero cost. Nor is it about flash plug-ins, dancing hamsters, or video over mobile phones. Indeed there are those who feel that the "e" in e-marketing is so misleading that it should be replaced with an "i" because it is the interactivity of the medium that makes it so special; the opportunity to establish dialogue with consumers.

The problem is that, reasonably enough given decades of mass media, there has been a concerted attempt by media and marketing companies to treat the Net as simply another medium; a very slow form of television, or radio with added text and pictures. Even that, however, is an improvement on the early 1990s when advertising and marketing companies did their level best to deny that the Net existed in any meaningful way at all.

In 1994 when the first banner ads were making their appearance the major advertising agencies were uninformed and often dismissive with regard to the Web. In the UK there is a stock question to see how "real-world" someone is, which is to ask them the price of a pint of milk. In a variation on that, *Campaign*, the advertising industry newspaper, did a call around to find out if agencies knew how much a Website cost. The answers came back instantly, glib, and high, but without any details as to how the figures were reached. Which was understandable, really. The perception from clients was that a Website was a marketing necessity, a box that had to be ticked, and thus turned to their advertising agencies and demanded answers

Agencies, however, were far more familiar with the worlds of TV and print, and in turn farmed out the work to a new breed of multimedia company. These companies were always small, often creatively driven, and usually entirely free of any marketing specialists. They delivered Websites, screensavers, CD-ROMs, and games as requested, but because they were separate from the client's main marketing machine it often took a long time for the real potential of the medium to get through. The issue of judging how much and how well people interacted with the material was often poorly understood.

EYEBALLS, HITS, COOKIES AND MORE

At that time it was still marketing currency to evaluate a Website's success in terms of "hits." A hit was registered when a user visited a page, which meant that the marketers could claim a new pair of eyes had seen their message. Talk of the hunt for "eyeballs" became all the rage.

Hits were a wildly inaccurate measure of customer interest, however, because a hit was registered for each element of the page that was viewed. A page with lots of pictures on it registered a hit for each image that loaded, which meant that one confused mess, briefly glimpsed and then abandoned, could score many times more than a single message that was digested and appreciated.

By 1995 the industry was getting savvy to this, and Websites were increasingly being measured by "page impressions," meaning one score for each whole page viewed by the customer. Banner adverts were scored by "clickthroughs" – the number of times users clicked on the ad to be transported to the promoter's site. CPM (Cost Per Mille, i.e. one thousand clicks) came to be established as a pricing structure.

What's important here is not the commercialization of the Web as a medium, but the growing realization that its value lay in precise reporting. The nature of electronic media, that all-important "e," meant that very exact pictures could be built up of the behavior both of customers in general, and individual consumers in particular. Advertisements and pages, it was realized, could be used to set "cookies"; little tags recorded to the individual user's computer. These cookies identified where a user had been, and could be used to target marketing ever more closely. It was now possible to recognize a keen fisherman, or boating enthusiast, simply by knowing where they'd been before. Having automatically identified them it was possible to serve up ads suitable for that individual.

The realization of that was one of the reasons for Poppe Tyson spinning off its ad sales unit as a separate company called DoubleClick that specialized in setting cookies, and tracking patterns. DoubleClick is not the only agency of its kind to offer such services to marketers at large, but its formation was a step towards solving one of advertising's great problems. It is a longstanding joke in the industry that every marketer knows that half their budget is completely wasted. The point is that no one knows just which half. The "e" factor in e-marketing now held the mouth-watering promise of solving that conundrum; of telling marketers just who looked at what, and what they did afterwards. The problem that became clear however, was that what people wanted to do was to completely ignore advertisements.

DOWN COMES THE BANNER

The extraordinary reporting and tracking abilities offered by the medium meant that the industry could be left in no doubt that by 1998 the banner format was in serious decline. Not that it was an endangered species in terms of numbers – indeed it was breeding faster than small mammals – nor in terms of finance (though that was to come in the aftermath of the bursting of the dotcom bubble). No, the decline was far more serious – it was a decline in clickthroughs. Quite simply, people were avoiding advertisements, rarely clicking on them despite the fact that ads now boasted animation and even limited video. The advent of pop-ups (separate windows that pop up with a marketing message as you browse a page) and interstitials (messages that appear while a chosen page is still loading) only seemed to exacerbate consumer frustration with broadcast-style advertising – what Seth Godin in his book *Permission Marketing* refers to as "interruption marketing": "Originally, the Internet captured the attention of interruption marketers. They rushed in, spent billions of dollars applying their interruption marketing techniques and discovered almost total failure."

The decline of the banner ad is well documented. By 1999 the *E-Marketer Advertising Report* declared that "banners, which accounted for 52% of all advertising on the Internet in 1998, will decrease considerably, representing only 26% of Web advertising sales by 2001." The report noted that advertising dollars from banner ads were in the process of migrating to strategic sponsorships. Tumbling clickthrough rates (down to about 0.3% at the time of writing) suggested that treating the Web simply as another mass medium was just not working. Interruption marketing was proving difficult in a medium in which a simple click would close down an unwanted window, and banners were clearly proving very easy to ignore altogether.

By the year 2000 then, less than four years after the Web had come to the attention of advertising agencies, it was becoming clear that attempting to treat it as simply another publishing or broadcasting medium was only creating a situation of diminishing returns. Ever inventive, the industry has started to explore ways of prolonging the life of the banner.

One of the problems was perceived to be the degree of interruption. The main purpose of a banner ad was seen as driving traffic – the user's attention is caught by the ad, they click on it, and are transported to the client's home page. The point of that was very quickly appreciated by advertising agencies since the site statistics would clearly show the client how many "eyeballs" the agency's ad had brought to them.

Still remaining, however, was the problem that a well-placed ad gains attention precisely because it is on a site that interests the user who is therefore unlikely to want to leave. This is why many marketers are now exploring the possibilities of "rich media" banners that not only animate or display video, but allow a user to interact entirely within them. In some cases it is possible to conduct a transaction and make a purchase all within a banner ad superimposed on a popular Web page. That way they don't leave the site that caught their eye in the first place.

Buying keywords is another trend on the increase in an attempt to make banner ads better targeted and thus increase clickthrough. In keyword buying, an oven manufacturer, for example, pays a search engine to "own" a word such as "cooking" for a set period of time. Whenever that word is typed into the search engine our oven maker's advertisement will pop up on the results page. Trying to make such ads more relevant, and capable of interaction themselves is, critics argue, simply trying to extend the life of a whole approach to marketing that appears to be staring at its sell-by date.

CONSUMER LEVERAGE

Instead, the adherents of *Permission Marketing*, *Relationship Marketing*, and *One-to-One Marketing* point to the Web as the single greatest tool ever invented for managing customer relations.

One of the features of the Web is that individuals on it can very easily form up and create chat rooms or Websites which then become forums for discussion. That ability to organize and amplify opinion has often proved daunting for business, not least since it provides an instant home for dissatisfied customers and complaints about product flaws. "It sucks" sites have sprung up everywhere complaining (legitimately or otherwise) about products and companies. No one is immune, least of all the companies that enable people to take part in the online communities – the proof of which is the existence of the site www.AOLsucks.com which details gripes and technical glitches for the world's largest ISP. In the past, companies either tried to ignore the conversations going on about them or else squash them by trying to have the sites closed down.

Both approaches are legacies of a media landscape that could be controlled by a limited number of publishers and broadcasters. Online, however, each consumer is also a publisher and an "It sucks" site can very easily have the apparent weight, not to mention the traffic, of the manufacturer's home page.

On the other hand, far from making Canute-like efforts to gag that flow of information, some marketers have harnessed its potential, notably with viral campaigns such as that for Hotmail, the Blair Witch, and AI (see Chapters 6 & 7 of this title). Consultants Burson-Marsteller believe they have identified a profile of online influencers, dubbed e-fluentials, who while numbering around 8% of the (US) Internet population, nonetheless have the power to influence the decisions of a further 72 million Americans. "In the old economy – or the offline world – one person was generally thought to have an impact on the attitudes and behavior of approximately two people," notes Christopher Komisarjevsky, president and CEO of Burson-Marsteller Worldwide. "However in the new economy, one influential online person has an impact on the attitudes and behavior of approximately eight people. The challenge today and in the future will be for companies, communities, and government agencies to understand e-fluentials and harness their potential impact to achieve measurable business results in this new e-society." Clearly e-marketers can be added to Komisarjevsky's list of those facing the new challenges.

Third generation telephony, interactive TV, and broadband will all make it possible for marketers to employ ever richer and more attractive-looking messages in the near future (see Chapter 6). The danger here is that the ability to use video more extensively will help perpetuate the image of the Net and its associated electronic devices as being another broadcast medium. It is not, and the decline of the banner ad should serve as a warning to those who feel it can be treated as such.

The e-dimension to e-marketing is an awareness that the medium no longer goes simply from broadcaster/advertiser to consumer. Nor is it just that there is a back channel for simple feedback and purchasing requests. The real e-dimension is about the links that are now created between all the consumers themselves, and the power and information that these give them. It is harnessing that dimension, whatever the technology it happens to use, that will prove the real task for the e-marketer of tomorrow.

A "BEST PRACTICE" EXAMPLE

Back in 1996 *Advertising Age* magazine singled out Ogilvy & Mather as the best advertising agency in adopting the Web as part of its media outlook. While all of the major agencies have come in for criticism for their initial refusal to take the Web seriously, Ogilvy has done a great deal since to recover lost ground; but in doing so have had to face the issues of media integration.

"New media" marketing evolved in isolation from its more established counterparts for a number of reasons. Initially undervalued, the new media aspect of a campaign was rarely seen as a major issue for standard marketing departments or media planners and so was farmed out. Even when the revenues involved meant that media planners and marketers took note, they still continued to treat it as a specialty, the responsibility of a separate online department, which didn't help with campaign integration. Aside from cultural attitudes towards the upstart medium the technical nature of it inclined it to be a specialist issue simply because it required so much learning just to stay ahead of the curve.

Ogilvy & Mather was one of the first to try and incorporate new media into the general mix, an achievement that seems to have had as much to do with its clients as its clairvoyance. Tim Carrigan, founder of Ogilvy Interactive (the e-marketing division of the agency) explains that: "The big Ogilvy thing came from its relationship with IBM. Early in 1995 both companies could see that the Net was an important marketing vehicle for IBM and from that they saw the potential for all their clients." Indeed IBM and Ogilvy saw e-marketing as a key tool for conquering a "new market" idea, that of e-business. The resulting campaign dominated the Net, as well as traditional media including TV ads. "Ask consumers who they associate with e-business and they say 'IBM'," notes Carrigan, " – the company has been very successful in establishing ownership of that idea."

Being in at the beginning has helped the agency stay ahead: "The good thing about getting involved early is that we went through the learning curve early and we have that knowledge internally," says Carrigan. "It's proved harder for agencies entering the market later, and who still find themselves exploring uncharted territory." That advance has seen some notable mixed media successes for other clients too, including American Express, whose new "Blue" credit card needed to establish its Web credentials (it offers guaranteed secure shopping online) and so embarked on combined TV and Web campaigns.

"The philosophy," Carrigan explains, "is one of 360 degree branding. Traditionally companies have fragmented their budgets on branding or marketing, and in the process the different marketing elements are no longer driven from the same understanding of the brand or the objectives. What we're trying to do as a company is to say that you can put all those together and manage them as one. That way whether it's Net ads, or the response of a call center, TV, or the feeling you get just walking into the company building – every single point of contact for the consumer in fact – the brand message should be consistent. It's certainly not about bolting on e-marketing at the last minute – about having a few geeks who you hand a TV commercial to and tell them to put it on the Net. Instead, if you take the IBM example you have to think that if IBM is all about e-business, then how does that affect the way it relates to customers in every context – whether that's in the mail or on a WAP phone. At Ogilvy Interactive we work across any interactive touch points, current or emerging, and our job is to manage the brand in those interactive channels providing a "joined-up" experience.

KEY INSIGHTS

The key to the World Wide Web is not that a marketer can reach millions, it's that those millions all have access to each other. The market's ability to reply to a message rivals that of the marketer in sending it out, making the medium more suited to dialogue than to dictation. This in turn can cause problems for marketers who are used to traditional mass media, and so associate marketing as being the message they want to get out, not as a process of listening to the audience.

This cultural shift then has notable implications within organizations too, as marketing departments and online specialists tend to work in isolation from each other with resulting misunderstandings and a lack of overall consistency in message. The companies who appear to be combating this best are those with a more holistic approach, integrating new media specialists into the marketing departments and having them involved in the early stages.

The Global Dimension

Implications and issues of globalization:

» the global online population;
» cultural issues – losing something in translation;
» legal issues; and
» best practice.

MORE THAN JUST NUMBERS

J. Walter Thompson, the largest foreign advertising agency in China, used to have a home page which kicked off by impressing the visitor with the mind-boggling statistics of that country's population. It then expressed the marketer's standard reaction as "what if I could sell one bar of soap to every one of those people." The point JWT wanted to get across to its potential clients was that thinking about it in those terms was an illusion, there was no uniform nation, and the market in question was a whole country, not just a mathematical entity. As if to make that point further JWT has since revamped the whole site as an educational introduction to the history and diversity of the country.

Just as most marketers approached China thinking: "Wow, just how many consumers is that?" there is the danger of being blinded by the figures for the World Wide Web and seeing it as one homogeneous group of people. A mathematical entity, a hypothetical number of soap bars sold. It's not a surprising response – we are forever being told of globalization, global reach, and global markets, so you might well expect a global marketing campaign. Furthermore a massive historical bias meant that since the Web began its commercial life in North America it was seen to be an American phenomenon, and as such one that spoke English and adhered to Western ideals. The extraordinary onward march of the Web continues apace.

The *First Quarter 2001 Global Internet Trends* report from Nielsen//NetRatings (www.nielson-netratings.com) looked at 27 countries around the world and found that over 420 million people now have Internet access. True, some 41% of that audience is to be found in the US and Canada, but the tide is shifting as the figures for Europe, Middle East and Africa (27%) and Asia Pacific (20%) grow. In response to those figures Richard Goosey, chief of analytics at ACNielsen eRatings.com commented: "Don't expect this American domination to last long, though. Compared with a year ago, significantly more households in Europe and Asia Pacific now have a PC in the home and a greater proportion of homes are making use of that PC to connect to the Internet. Over the next 12 months, another 9% of European households and 12% of Asia Pacific households plan on acquiring Internet access." As if in confirmation a report by *eMarketer* estimates that West and East

European users combined will outnumber North Americans as early as 2002.

Contrary to popular wisdom the world is not a small place. With over 230 countries (an ever-changing figure), more than 6,700 languages (again open to dispute), and hundreds of currencies (although this figure at least looks to be shrinking), globalization is not going to be a smooth process for the marketer. Set against that is the fact that e-commerce has shattered the entry barriers for international trade. The Web is a shop window on the world, and for the sake of creating a site, a banner ad, or even just an e-mail it is possible for the e-marketer to spread the message well beyond national boundaries. The fact that the number of e-mail "boxes" outside the US is now believed to have exceeded the number within it also adds impetus. Any e-marketer not already doing so can now count the days before someone suggests they launch an international campaign.

If proof were needed that campaigns can spread widely, and wildly, across borders then surely there is nothing better than the spectacle of young French roller-bladers greeting each other in the Bois de Boulogne with the Budweiser "Waaassup." The phenomena of Flat Eric and Pikachu have likewise made a laughing stock of linguistic or political barriers. For every such success, however, there are hordes of lesser campaigns that stutter and die away, victims of an inability to consider the cultural and even legal issues that underpin national identities.

MIND YOUR LANGUAGE

Language issues are often more a source of embarrassment and amusement than serious offence. Poorly translated messages inevitably take on an air of amateurishness, and yet to this day major companies entrust the translation of online messages to people who are not native speakers of the target language, and if they are native speakers, rarely have any experience of marketing or copywriting.

One of the biggest sources of problems comes with product names, sometimes because they are already in use for a different product, sometimes because they have an unexpected translation. Technology company Creative Labs was confident that with its Nomad MP3 music player it had a name and image that would travel easily. Unfortunately in France the name is in use by a mobile telecoms company – a situation which would have caused problems for that campaign (wisely it was cancelled).

Simple product confusion is the least of the international marketer's worries. There have been worse cases which should surely raise not just eyebrows but questions at board level. What was Vauxhall (General Motors in the US) thinking when it released a car across Europe called the Nova (literally "won't go" in Spanish). Or Ford, who released both the Caliente ("hooker" in Mexican slang), and Pinto which in Brazilian slang not only means the male organ, but a small one at that. In London the throat lozenge Zubes were widely advertised with the slogan "Go suck on a Zube." Zube is slang for penis throughout the Arab-speaking world – a fact pointed out when double-decker buses carrying the message passed by the Arabic communities of Bayswater.

From President Kennedy announcing to the inhabitants of Berlin that he was a type of doughnut (the local translation of "ich bin ein Berliner"), key messages have always lost much in translation. Pepsi's translation of "Come alive with the Pepsi generation" has unfortunately been rendered in Chinese as "Pepsi brings your ancestors back from the dead," and Braniff airline's proud boast about its upholstery – "Fly in Leather" – sounded even more enticing when translated into Spanish with the alternative meaning of "Fly naked."

Even when the site is in English it is important to remember the difference between English as spoken by a native, and clear, comprehensible English by those for whom it is a second language. There is a useful article on the need for international English by Susan Solomon entitled "Apology to Kazakhstan" at the Clickz site (www.clickz.com/author/auth199.html). Unfortunate names and poor translation aside, the unwary e-marketer can fall foul of some surprising cultural differences.

KEEPING OUT OF COURT

German marketing laws are notably strict when it comes to price descriptions, and in a bid to eradicate confusing price information they have outlawed anything that might confuse customers about the price of an item. Likewise, in order to avoid fraudulent claims by suggesting massive reductions from non-existent list prices the law also controls the degree by which anything can be discounted. Which means that even if correctly translated and spelt, the familiar phrase "two for the price of one" is forbidden in Germany, as is "half price" or "40% off." Use of any of these in a banner or marketing message appearing in Germany could lead the unwitting e-marketer into court.

Jurisdictional barriers are also proving a potential headache as recent events in France have shown. The French courts ruled that Yahoo was breaking French law by having Nazi memorabilia on sale on its auction sites. No matter that the material might be advertised by those outside the French border, the fact that it was therefore on sale in France meant that it was adjudged to fall under French law and the company was obliged to prohibit access to it.

On the same basis marketers would have to be very careful about ensuring that marketing messages and images complied with the moral and legal standards of the countries they were seen in. Think for a moment about the fact that for Saudi Arabia, for example, that would mean ensuring that no images in your campaign featured a woman driving or smoking a cigarette.

PAYMENT PROBLEMS

Even when you have sorted out your translations, weeded out any cross-cultural innuendo or misunderstandings, complied with foreign marketing laws, and ensured that your messaging is culturally harmonious, there may still be the issue of payment. The advent of the euro should make life easier there, with a single currency for non-Europeans to deal with; and yet for the e-marketer there still remain problems when it comes to online transactions.

The prospect of a single currency may hold tantalizing promise of price transparency – instant like-for-like comparison of costs for goods and services – but it is unlikely to make all the countries of Europe equal at a stroke. A recent report on European e-tailers by research company Forrester (www.forrester.com) concluded that the degrees of regulation and payment practices in each country had a significant affect on the national markets for online shopping.

The UK and Sweden, both relatively regulation-light, provide the most liberal environment for e-commerce, whereas the strict laws of Southern Europe and Germany on pricing promotions and discounts do little to encourage buying, selling, and marketing online. Those countries with a strong attachment to plastic also take to e-commerce more easily than those with a cash culture. In Europe the Swedes, Swiss, Spaniards, and Italians prefer using hard cash for transactions. The French and Germans still use a great many checks, and areas of Switzerland prefer to have an invoice submitted for payment. Only UK consumers follow US trends and include credit cards among their top three favorite ways to pay. Coping with the local preferred method of payment is not usually a priority for expanding e-commerce operations, which typically presume that as long as they take Visa and Mastercard they have covered all the options.

SOME OTHER GLOBAL ISSUES

Web penetration is an obvious factor to take into account, but care is advised when looking into the numbers. According to the annual "Face of the Web" study by researchers Ipsos-Reid (www.ipsosreid.com) Western Europe (primarily the big four of the UK, France, Germany, and Italy) plus Australia, Canada, and South Africa form a bloc that rivals the US in terms of Internet use. South Korea and Singapore, both at over 45% Internet penetration, have more users per head of population than Germany, Belgium, or the UK (all at around 35%).

Ensuring that you're comparing like-with-like isn't just as simple as checking out the big figures. The way that consumers interact with information will also be affected by whether they are online at home or at work. Country-by-country statistics generally agree on much higher access levels at home than at work, but no two countries are the same when it comes to the exact numbers. In the Netherlands, for example, where home access has been boosted by cheap broadband thanks to cable, 56% of users have Internet access from home, but only 28% at work. 56% of Singaporeans can also surf from home in the high-tech city state, although a mere 21% have access by day from work. Denmark has an even higher proportion of people surfing from home with 58% of the population wired up, of whom a full 38% can also get online at work.

Another point often forgotten is the effect of time zones. Of course the Web is a famously 24/7 operation, but if you are going to begin conversation with the market then a 12-hour time difference means your service staff will always appear to wait at least a day before dealing with sales requests or customer information.

Last but not least, for all the spectacular growth figures it is still worth remembering that at least one out of every four people in China, India, Russia and the Third World have yet to hear of the Internet, and less than one tenth of the world's population is online.

POINTERS TOWARDS BEST PRACTICE

In e-marketing, as in so much else, the trusty slogan "think global, act local" still holds true. As much as the Web and its associated technologies seem to hold the key to effortless globe trotting, the international barriers of language, culture, and marketing law are still there, waiting to trip the trotter up. There is no substitute for local knowledge of a market, and there are endless half-cocked campaigns and page after page of shabbily translated marketing material to attest to that fact. Since enlisting the help of good local knowledge will involve time and effort, this also means that before "going global" a good marketer is going to start by thinking big, then narrowing it down.

First choose your market

Why would you want to narrow it down when the whole world's your oyster? Because you're unlikely to be able to hold meaningful conversation with most of the world, and if you're not doing that then you're just shouting your message – adding to the media noise. Before going global, try and ask yourself:

» Which countries would have most strategic value to my company?
» With which would I be most likely to achieve meaningful conversation?
» Which countries should I actively rule out, making it clear that my company is not trying to sell to them?

The first of these questions is dependent on what your products or services are. It may be wise to remember the J. Walter Thompson argument and avoid being stuck in the soap-selling mindset of "one head of population = a sale." There's more to a good "fit" than throwing campaigns at the most populous countries, or those with the highest earnings per capita.

Obtain local knowledge

Having chosen countries or regions that appeal, take local advice – which may possibly mean hiring local representation or going to an agency. Too many companies have regretted believing they could skip that step and save money. Things that you need to learn from local expertise include the following:

» Language – yes, of course you've thought of that one, but have you checked with a local speaker? English and Americans allegedly speak the same language but you only have to ask either about "buns," "fanny-bags," "fags," or "pants" to realize the potential for local language confusion.
» Law. Consumer law varies enormously from country to country, so do you fall under that country's law with regard to such things as, say, return policies? Privacy laws likewise vary enormously – the EU directive on privacy aims to make it illegal to gather information in EU countries and then return it to the US where there is no equivalent of the Data Protection Act. Marketing laws, such as those in Germany, may be beyond the imagination of the marketer used to US/UK approaches.
» Payment preferences. Every payment system claims to be accepted all over the world, and yet anyone who's ever tried to pay with American Express in France will tell you that payment preferences vary enormously from country to country.

Consumer and cultural issues

This is not simply a matter of checking that your image of a cow isn't offensive to locals; it's also a matter of researching another cultural subset – that of local online culture. Countries vary enormously as to whether surfing is done at home, or at the office. Access speeds are not only dependent on ISDN, DSL, or cable penetration, but also whether telco monopolies charge high prices for them or whether local competition has paved the way for cheap broadband.

Keep listening

Having studied the market, taken that local advice, and implemented a campaign, be prepared to go back and listen to local suggestions whenever things don't seem to be running to plan. If markets are conversations there is little scope in being a bad listener, or worse, paying mere lip service to local issues or feelings.

KEY INSIGHTS

» The "world wide" in "www" increasingly means exactly what it says.

» The world is not composed entirely of English speakers.

» Even where English is spoken it may not be spoken in the same way as elsewhere.

» A translation service is not all that is required to cater for another market – laws, customs, consumer behavior, even the colors used on a Website all have to be considered

» Local knowledge is invaluable, and those who felt it unnecessary to confer locally have often fallen foul of hurdles they couldn't see.

» The fact that you *can* embark on a global campaign doesn't necessarily mean that you *should*.

» Think global, act local.

The State of the Art

Current debate on such subjects as:

» permission marketing;
» viral marketing;
» m-commerce and wireless marketing;
» interactive TV; and
» key insights.

OPTING IN, OPTING OUT

"From time to time we offer to share our list of subscribers with door-to-door aromatherapy salespersons and ritual axe-murderers. If you would prefer that your data not be used in this way, please check the box."

Christopher Locke, The ClueTrain Manifesto

One of the key battles of the moment is being fought over that most insignificant-looking element of a Web page – the little check boxes that ostensibly allow customers to opt in or out of receiving further information, or having their details passed on to someone else. It's sometimes hard to understand what all the fuss is about – after all, on the face of it a check box couldn't be simpler. Like a light switch the check box is a binary device – it can only have one of two states; yes/no, on/off, in/out.

Unfortunately the question to which people are replying "yes" or "no" to is not always the same. Asking you to click on a box to request more information is relatively clear permission to send marketing material, but what about asking you to click on that box in order *not* to receive the information? Or, one step further; what if the box is already checked asking for more information, and the customer is expected to find it and uncheck it if they *don't* want more information? Expecting customers to do something, usually to click on a box to check or uncheck it, is called negative opt-in, or passive consent. Unfortunately what e-marketers may see as passive consent is also seen as sharp practice by a lot of users.

The initial appeal of opt-out to a marketer is obvious. A great way of harvesting prospective clients, it can also be proudly displayed to clients and peers as an example of "targeted marketing" – and of course it means the chance to build mailing lists which are potentially valuable either in use or as products to sell on. It is still remarkably common with examples cropping up all the time, including eMarketer.com's revelation that Microsoft, owner of Hotmail, was passing on subscriber e-mail addresses to the Internet White Pages at InfoSpace. In order *not* to have their details passed on customers had to – you guessed it – uncheck a box. Even online communities, supposedly well versed in their users' habits and likes, have been found doing the same thing.

GeoCities found itself on the receiving end of attention from the US Federal Trade Commission after it became clear that the company collected income and education information on its users, promising that it would not share this without permission. Permission, however, came in the form of a box that the user had to check. Surveys repeatedly show that consumers regard opt-out as undesirable, and the marketing material they receive if they fail to tick that box is consequently seen as spam (junk mail on the Internet).

For believers in permission marketing the opt-in approach enjoys further added weight since it matches better with guru Seth Godin's definition of such marketing as being relevant (since the customer has actively expressed interest) and anticipated (in that you hope the customer is looking forward to receiving that information). Common sense also dictates that a customer who actively chooses to learn more is a more valuable prospect than someone who simply failed to check a box, possibly because they hadn't realized they had to. According to NOP (National Opinion Polls) research, 87% of UK consumers find unsolicited commercial e-mail unacceptable. By contrast, 48% of consumers are willing to give their e-mail address to a Website in order to receive targeted advertising on a subject of interest to them.

Many opt-out schemes also add injury to insult by failing to make it easy for a customer to unsubscribe if they do find they are receiving unwanted mail. Unsubscribe information should be clear, and prefer-ably consist of no more than a URL or a hyperlink, rather than make a customer go through any more detailed reply system. What really annoys customers, the author included, is when that unsubscribe system doesn't then work, it continues to send spam but has the addition to the address that you are now customer@unsubscribe.company.com.

Despite resistance to opt-out approaches they are still popular, and still supported by direct marketing organizations including the UK's DMA (Direct Marketing Association).

Leaving aside the ethical and quality based arguments, there are also a couple of practical and legislative issues that e-marketers need to be aware of. The first is the existence of the Mail Abuse Prevention System, which compiles a list of companies accused of sending spam.

That list, imaginatively entitled the Realtime Blackhole List, is then supplied to ISPs who wish to use it to protect their customers – often by blocking mail coming from those servers. Marketing companies, even self-professed permission marketers, have found themselves or their servers included on that list, and once on it is extremely hard to be removed or to restore a good name. Perhaps unsurprisingly then, there is criticism of the opt-out approach in the online industry itself. In the UK Mailtrack, a specialist in building and managing permission-based email databases, polled 180 ISPs and found that 98% of them strongly favor an opt-in policy rather than the opt-out approach.

The other key point is that in line with a recent EU directive many European countries (including the UK with its updated Data Protection Act) now have legislation that defines exactly how customer data can be held and used. The rules restrict the type of data that can be gathered, the time it can be held, and to whom it can be passed on. Most importantly they stipulate that it can under no circumstances be passed on to a company in a country where there is no such protection. The US is the prime example of such a country, so if a UK subsidiary of a US company passes back information it may be in breach of the law. In the US, while there is no directly comparable law, there is legislation protecting users from unsolicited mail and specifying that all mail must have a reply address and be able to get off the list (whether or not they failed to tick a box).

In order to gain some idea of the potential scope of this problem, consider that by 2003, *eMarketer* estimates that 97% of all e-mail received will be some form of marketing, 75% of which will be unsolicited. If that becomes true then the power of e-mail marketing can only be severely undermined.

MARKETING SUCCESS CAN BE CATCHING

Although viral marketing is very much a modern buzzword, what it actually refers to is undoubtedly the oldest marketing technique on the planet. Viral marketing is nothing more complicated than word of mouth, and as such the term could be applied retrospectively to any information that is spread through personal endorsement or simply the "hey look at this" factor. The reason why the technique is of such importance to the e-marketer is that the speed and reach of the Net means that fast-breeding messages circle the globe more rapidly than bad news or celebrity scandal, quite possibly making fortunes in the process.

The term "viral marketing" itself is accredited to the venture capitalist who helped fund Hotmail (see Chapter 7: Success Stories), itself the best example of a company rocketed to success entirely by the new electronic word of mouth. Hotmail proved that by offering something of perceived value you could get customers to pass it on to their friends. According to a Jupiter Communications survey 81% of people who read viral messages pass them on to at least one other person, and nearly half will pass it on to two or three people. Nor is it just the obviously useful that gets passed on. Free e-mail was not only a novelty when Hotmail started its worldwide whispering campaign, it was also extremely practical and a way of helping friends keep in touch.

The benefits to some other lightning globetrotters has been less obvious; novelties such as the dancing hamster animation were passed on simply because of the "look at this" factor. The dancing baby phenomenon actually made it so big it crossed over from the Web and onto mainstream television making frequent appearances in the TV series *Ally McBeal*.

Many successful viral campaigns have capitalized on the success of novelties like the dancing baby animation. Screensavers, for example, are usually free to download, and then not only display upon the screen to which they were downloaded, but hopefully will attract the attention of others in the workspace. The user is a salesperson by power of suggestion and implicit personal endorsement, and the screensaver itself gets a chance to play to others and prove its worth (coolness, humor, etc.).

In the UK the Guinness screensaver, effectively a made-for-TV beer ad transformed into a very simple yet singing/dancing animation, quickly became the scourge of office managers everywhere. Others soon followed, and since novelty value is notoriously short-lived, screensavers quickly followed one after the other.

The problem for the marketer is that the bar is raised each time. Creating a genuinely funny or eye-catching sales message within the technical constraints of a screensaver is no mean piece of marketing, and success is both rare and fleeting. Likewise downloadable games that reinforce marketing messages are rightly popular since if they are attention-grabbing they will prove contagious in the office and popular to pass on amongst friends. There is no shortage of free games on the Net, however, and so it takes something pretty eye-catching to make the grade.

A difficulty with viral marketing is that every marketer would love to turn all their clients into salespeople, and in their haste to do so some have forgotten the reason why the best campaigns have worked. As we have seen it is hard work to come up with something so creative, so novel, or so obviously useful, that people will rush to pass it on. Many marketers have simply given up the struggle to do so and resorted instead to another tactic at least as old as word of mouth – bribery.

Bribery, in the form of incentives such as discounts and freebies, is a tried and trusted technique for getting people to surrender information about themselves. If they consider the offer good enough they will also recommend it to friends simply because we all like to do friends a favor. In the UK Virgin Net, the ISP arm of the Virgin empire, had 20,000 cinema tickets to give away – in return for which the company asked for them to register their names and details. According to Virgin Net publisher Alex Dale, the campaign started small – just ten e-mails were sent out suggesting they pass it on to their friends. Within three hours all 20,000 tickets were gone and a further 17,000 people registered for further information and promotions, even though they knew the tickets had long since been handed out.

Flushed with the success of that promotion, Virgin launched another viral campaign. Into your in-tray would come an e-mail telling you that one of your friends will invite you to Richard Branson's private Caribbean island with them if they win a prize holiday there. The person doesn't have to do anything else, just bask in the warm glow of that recommendation. If they wish to, however, they can follow the link to the quiz and increase their chances of winning the holiday (with their friend) by trying it for themselves. Of course that involves registering, and possibly adding the e-mail of another friend who might want to come, from which point the chain goes on.

Not all campaigns have respected that fine line between enlisting users and their friends as a sales force, and raising the suspicion that they are being exploited. Ikea withdrew a scheme in the San

Francisco area where site visitors could earn themselves discounts by e-mailing virtual postcards to friends. The postcard also offered the reductions to their friends, and the sender wasn't repaid on any kind of commission basis, but even so the offer was pulled after a number of people expressed discomfort. It was felt to be too close for comfort to the kind of sales recruitment scheme that leads to people pestering long-forgotten acquaintances in the attempt to sell them timeshares or insurance.

There is also the danger of opt-in/opt-out issues (see above) emerging in viral campaigns. Some companies have treated a referral as an opt-in, so that not only has the person passing on the message opted to receive more information, but so has the friend to whom they sent it. That approach is too akin to spam, especially if the receiver turns out to be simply another name on a mailing list group with little or no contact with the referrer. If a viral campaign can't generate enough interest to drive new recruits to the site to register and opt-in for themselves then the marketer behind it should think carefully about whether it is compelling enough to run.

TRADE IS IN THE AIR

M-commerce and with it m-marketing (the "m" meaning "mobile") is that branch of e-marketing that reaches out into the brave new world of wireless, be that using today's generation of mobile phones, WAP phones, wirelessly connected palmtops, or the next generations of telephony.

According to research company Gartner, every economically-active European citizen will own a mobile phone within four years; the number of mobile phones in the world will exceed 1 billion by 2003; and the average penetration of data-enabled mobile phones in the European Union will surpass 65% of the population by 2004.

The great promise of the world of wireless is that not only does it serve up a known individual on their mobile phone/wireless PDA etc. but also it does so at a known time, and best of all at a known place. Future generations of mobile phones will have far more precise locating technology, but even with the cellphones of today it is possible for the network to pin someone down to within a few hundred yards in most cities. That in turn makes it possible to automatically offer certain services. Tourists in Florence, Italy, for example, may be surprised to note that as they near the historic center, their phone messages them to offer tourist information or multilingual tours.

The system is simply a function of existing capability – the phone is identified as foreign when it hooks up to the local network, and its owner's home country is clear from the roaming agreement between the two networks. Triggering the message is simply a function of recognizing when that cell phone enters the range of the cell antennae in the city center.

In Finland, pioneering home of mobile telephony, such services are commonplace. For example, hard liquor can only be bought from state-controlled outlets, so it is common for the thirsty Finn to type in a demand for the nearest shop. The network checks his location and replies with a text message giving driving or walking instructions.

The great explosion in such services was expected to be WAP (Wireless Application Protocol); a means of allowing mobile phones to interrogate and get data from web sites. The idea was that by hooking up to a local listings site, for example, a businessman visiting a new town could instantly find restaurants, cinemas, and hotels. There is even a case of a parking meter manufacturer announcing the possibility of parking meters so you could use your phone to find a free space. If you combine database marketing with the individual ID of each phone/wireless device, and their geographical location, you would then be perfectly placed to offer them relevant services.

Two big problems loom large with this scenario. The first is that the work of linking up database marketing with the positioning is tricky technically, and just plain hard work in the human sense. There are manufacturers talking of building a satellite-based GPS (Global Positioning System) into handsets but in the meantime the information comes from working out the nearest receiving point to the phone. That information is pretty much the privilege of the particular network being used, which makes it very difficult to create a system that can match up any user in any place regardless of which phone network they use. Because there has been no real tailoring of information, or much use of geographical location, the messages sent out to date have largely been generic, or relied on the user opting to look at listings pages culled from the Web. Which has so far proved less than compelling.

The second problem is the fear of just what would happen if all that hard work were done, and e-marketers could pinpoint a customer's location, cross-referenced with that person's profile. I have heard it earnestly suggested that someone walking down a street could have their phone targeted with offers and best buys from every shop they walk past. Technically possible, perhaps, but what consumer would want it? Irresponsible or insensitive marketing is likely to prove even more of a headache in the mobile world than in conventional media, not least since the fact that the devices are so personal means there is the risk of unwanted invasion of privacy. We've all suffered from spam e-mails or junk mail through the door; now imagine if the phone in your pocket or the pager in your purse was besieged all day with pizza promotions and coupons for online shopping.

There are developments that look promising, however. Broadband mobile telephony (often called third generation or 3G) is on its way, despite the setback to would-be operators of the high costs of buying the licenses in European countries. With 3G the prospect of animation and even video comes into play, offering greater potential for the smart marketer to produce marketing material that engages the customer. Who knows, if it's good enough we may even see opt-in m-campaigns.

Another development is the way phones are starting to be used. In Japan, where 3G is already in place, one of the success areas has proved to be gaming with the possibility of modifying and uploading game characters which can then be downloaded by others. At the same time in Europe (again largely thanks to the Finns) participation games are being played in which players roam the streets, receiving messages on their phones about the whereabouts of rivals. They use their handsets to activate "weapons" and by taking a look at the real-world location and time of both handsets the network decides whether or not they have scored hits. This development of the phone as plaything potentially takes the wireless device into the arena where entertaining viral campaigns such as games and screensavers come into play.

The technologies are new and untested, the installed base remains relatively low (but rising), and the vagaries of the markets mean that the high-tech marketers most likely to push into this area are not always as sure of their budgets as they were a year or two back. In addition to those factors the fear of failure is (rightly) high since there is a very real danger of being perceived as intrusive when sending messages to what is after all a very personal device. Nonetheless the explosive growth of mobile devices, and the applications for them, means that at some point wireless is likely to be the future battleground for the smarter e-marketer.

THE WIDENING SCOPE OF TV

Interactive TV is a misleading term simply because it is taken to mean some very different things. To the film distributors and rental outlets it's commonly seen to mean video on demand; to sports broadcasters it means "control" over camera shots. To marketers it ideally means clicking on something on screen in order to be served up with more information or even a chance to buy. Unfortunately early trials have also left much of the public with the impression that interactive TV means quiz shows with cardboard sets and the chance to press one of three buttons to answer a question.

In the confusion about the future of TV there have been any number of assertions put forward. Demos at trade shows have suggested that you would be able to click on any product on screen in a film to buy it (those demos have been showing for years now) to the idea that the PVR (Personal Video Recorder) means the death of ad revenues from TV. The thinking behind that one is that personalized recording services such as TiVo enable viewers to catch automatically every episode of their favorite programs.

Program time is no longer an issue – the device interrogates a Web-based listings schedule to find your favorite shows and saves them to disk whenever they appear. Tell the system you like ice hockey or stamp collecting and it will go away and try to find programs that match your request. What makes advertisers nervous is that the result is culled from any channel or time slot without the viewer knowing or caring, and it is taken without any of the ads before or after (or even in between in some systems). The end is nigh, say the doom-mongers.

Except that it's not. While the advent of TiVo and its rivals is one of the digital developments in TV, the interlinking of the Web and TV is another. Digital TV is with us now; indeed, in the UK analogue TV is due to be switched off altogether in a year or two, which means that the set-top box or integrated digital TV will be a part of home life. What interests marketers here is that these boxes are linked up to the Web, meaning that they can receive e-mails to the TV screen; and most importantly they can also send information back.

Digital TV can be delivered by cable, by satellite or terrestrially but for the moment the "back" or "return" channel usually means a phone line connection. This means that it's not fast – but that doesn't have to mean that it's not clever.

With a back channel in place it becomes relatively simple to introduce "click to order" ads. The system has full knowledge of the user, including billing information, so a simple banner saying "click now to buy" means that viewers don't even have to lift the phone to make the purchase. Simplistic, perhaps, but Domino pizza placed an ad on RespondTV back in 1999 that let *Star Trek* viewers click now to order couch potato fodder. The result was an astonishing 23% response rate.

Going one step beyond the basic "click to order" it is possible to have "click to inform" approaches where a click on the banner or pop-up button takes the viewer to a complementary Website with further information, which could be product data or character/theme-related backgrounders and games. Again the importance to the marketer is that the subscriber information, tied to Web reporting tools, makes it possible to build a very detailed picture of likes and dislikes.

Going further still is the grail of the enhanced video with which users can interact, including the idea of clicking on products or a character's clothing in order to get more information or a chance to buy. Exponents of this technique point to such ventures as AsSeenIn.com, a site that enables surfers to buy items similar to those being worn by their onscreen heroes. The idea of a live tie-up makes obvious sense.

The problems with all this stem from the fact that the different service providers in each country are still fighting the turf war. Most systems don't actually offer full Internet access, preferring instead a "walled garden" approach of limited content. This reassures family subscribers, but also gives the service provider a great deal of control, and means that "click to inform" or enhanced video might well have to be developed separately for each supplier's service.

In theory interactive TV provides the platform for the one-to-one credo and the power of mass media to come together. In practice the lack of technology standards, the struggles between rival formats and players (Sky, Microsoft, AOL...), and the relative immaturity of marketing material for the medium look set to dog interactive TV for some time. To that you can add the financial headaches of switching to digital. Currently the aspirant providers are heavily subsidizing the cost of set-top boxes which will have to be recouped from what is still a relatively small marketplace. It is these problems, more than the impact of PVRs that are most likely to trouble the e-marketer.

KEY INSIGHTS

» New technologies will always bring new challenges and opportunities for the e-marketer. An appreciation of their potential and limits will always be part of the job, even if an in-depth technical understanding may not be necessary

» As much as technology appears to dominate the agenda, the real industry conversations are really about best practice; a reflection, perhaps, of just how young an industry it is.

» Imposing the disciplines or tactics of another medium doesn't always work – direct mail marketers that cross the line into spam may well find themselves shut down or blocked – not something they will be familiar with from the traditional postal service.

» Whether using e-mail, viral campaigns, interactive TV, third generation phones or a faxback service, the success of e-marketing is measured by how well it engages the audience and how much they help spread the idea, rather than simply by totting up click-throughs or product sales.

E-Marketing in Practice:

Success Stories

Selected case studies from around the world:

» viral campaigns: Hotmail, AI;
» combined online/offline: Pepsi/Yahoo!;
» game and video viral marketing: Honda Civic, Johnny Walker Whisky;
» using banners for branding: British Airways; and
» e-mail marketing to convert browsers to shoppers: Reflect.com

HOTMAIL VIRAL CAMPAIGN

Whether or not Hotmail was the first viral e-mail marketing campaign is a moot point. What matters is that its remarkable success opened marketers eyes to the potential of e-mail campaigns, and led to the coining of the term "viral marketing" to describe the process. Unsophisticated by the standards of the campaigns that followed it, the growth of Hotmail still stands out not least because in a business that suffers from hype and vagueness in equal portions, the Hotmail story could point to two very hard facts indeed. One was the growth of a user base from zero to 12 million in just a year and a half (it now has over 30 million subscribers). The other was the fact that this was done with a marketing spend of less than $500 k.

Hotmail founders Sabeer Bhatia and Jack Smith had the idea for Hotmail after struggling to access their conventional e-mail accounts while on the move. Logging on via remote computers proved problematic, despite the fact that accessing the Web itself was increasingly easy, not least due to the mushrooming of Web cafes. Why not then create an e-mail service that was Web-based? All you had to do was go to a particular Website, accessible from any browser in the world, enter a personal password, and have access to your e-mails.

The two created the site, and the server technology that enabled them to offer these e-mails. Then, importantly, they hit on the financial model which was to offer the e-mail service entirely free to their users, and recoup revenue by offering advertising space on the pages. Having established the technology and the business model they were left to market the service.

The way they hit on to do this was simplicity itself – they would add an advertising tag line to every e-mail. Originally the suggestion was that each mail should carry the words "P.S. Get your free e-mail at Hotmail" as if the sender of the message was directly recommending the service. Hotmail baulked at the "P.S." with its suggestion of personal endorsement and pulled those two letters. That sensitivity to users' feelings is significant, and subsequent e-marketers would be wise to heed it. The message duly went out without the P.S. and the rest, as they say, is money in the bank.

The point was that every outbound message told the receiver that the sender used Hotmail, with the implicit suggestion that this new service offered a free means of keeping in touch with that sender, usually a friend or family member. Of course it didn't hurt that the basic product benefit, "free e-mail" was simple and easy to express.

Because they spread the messages and signed up to use the site themselves, every new user in effect became a sales agent for the service, and the sales network instantly spanned the globe, without any local marketing spend whatsoever. Nor was it just the young and broke who turned to it; there are tales of large corporates using it to satisfy their e-mail needs while their in-house systems went through the turmoil associated with mergers and acquisitions. Steven Jurvetson, of Draper Fisher Jurvetson, the venture capitalists that funded Hotmail, is credited with coining the phrase "viral marketing" to describe the process. "The definition keeps evolving," explained Jurvetson, "it's like an adaptive virus. We defined it initially as network-enhanced word of mouth. You turn every one of your customers into an involuntary salesperson for your company."

On July 4 1996 Hotmail was launched. Within a month it had reached 100,000 subscribers; in under six months it had passed the million mark. By the time subscriptions had reached 10 million the operation was not only causing concern at America Online, the world's largest e-mail provider, but was also attracting attention from Microsoft which bought out the company for a (reported) $400 mn. Figures for that sale vary but whatever you believe, it suffices to say that it made the two co-founders instant multimillionaires. According to the BBC the service now boasts 65 million users in over 220 countries around the world, making it one of the most popular online services ever.

Timeline

» **July 4 1996**: Hotmail is launched
» **August 1996**: subscriptions reach 100,000
» **By end 1997**: subscriptions approach 10 million
» **January 1998**: Hotmail is purchased by Microsoft
» **2001**: 65 million users in 220 countries

KEY INSIGHTS

The case of Hotmail shows just what can be done on the Web with a marketing budget of $500,000, and added the term "viral marketing" to the e-marketing lexicon. On a more prosaic level it also proved to be one of the fastest and most cost-efficient means of gathering a mailing list.

The key insights of the campaign are that if the incentive is good enough (in this case free e-mail) then the users themselves become the sales force. It also highlights the incredible speed of word of mouth on the Web, going from a user base of zero to 12 million in just a year and a half.

Perhaps most important of all, however, was the recognition, right from the start, that there is a fine line in such campaigns. Having their message spread by users worked like a dream, but the founders recoiled from the original idea of inserting it as if it was a P.S. from the sender. By respecting the fine line between being a user and being used, Bhatia and Smith stayed on the right side of online sentiment, and made a killing in the process.

AI VIRAL CAMPAIGN

The film world lives on buzz, particularly that generated around launches to ensure widespread awareness, interest, and ultimately opening weekend revenues. It's hardly surprising then that Hollywood should have proved quick off the mark in recognizing the potential for worldwide word of mouth.

Speed of digital communication and degree of connectivity means that a campaign that takes advantage of online bulletin boards and chat rooms can generate an enormous amount of awareness for a fraction of the cost of a poster campaign. That point was emphatically proved by the 1999 campaign for *The Blair Witch*, a budget horror released after an immensely successful yet shoestring "guerrilla" marketing campaign on the Net. Without a poster or trailer appearing, the film producers had created a site and a whispering campaign about it that meant introducing the subject in online discussions. It was claimed to be the first purely Net-based marketing campaign, a decision taken purely on budgetary considerations – makers Artisan Entertainment just didn't have the money for a conventional campaign. Aimed squarely at the 17–28 age group, it opted to spend the money on the Web. The film's Website had a budget of $15,000, but it received 75 million visits in the first week alone, and subsequently the film, produced for between $40,000 and $65,000 (estimates vary) and promoted with a total of less than $1.5 mn, took $79.7 mn on its first weekend.

More recently the approach was taken up and developed by Dreamworks, Steven Spielberg's studio for the advance campaign to accompany the film *AI* (Artificial Intelligence). *AI* started as a Stanley Kubrick production, based on a short story by Brian Aldiss called *Super Toys Last All Summer Long*. The story appeared in the 1960s and had been a Kubrick project for some time, but one which he held back in the belief that technology had yet to catch up with his vision for the film.

Spielberg's film, released in 2001, has already shown a mastery of media technology on the marketing side. The furore started when a short trailer was released on the Web. Sharp-eyed surfers noticed that its credits included the name Jeanine Salla, who is given the intriguing title of "sentient machine therapist." Curiosity aroused, many members of the online community turned to the popular search engine Google to enter the name and term to see what it turned up, exactly as the e-marketers had hoped. What the curious surfers then found was a link to the aforementioned Jeanine Sella at her job at the (fictitious) Bangalore World University as well as a host of personal home pages for her family.

Following the links, and calling phone numbers that appear on the sites (and are answered by answering machines) builds up a picture in which it becomes rapidly apparent that there is a close tie-in to another character called Evan Chan, who is dead. The mystery of his murder (?) takes users into a world in which the Sentient Property Crime Bureau hunts down robots that have broken the law, a world of robot slaves, robot resistance movements, anti-robot vigilante groups, and a series of Websites apparently set up by robots themselves. It is all the world of the film, though not the film's plot itself – rather what is called "back story" – a parallel plot line adding depth to the fictional universe. It would appear to consist of some 50 separate sites including contact points where users who enter their e-mail or fax get communications and clues sent to them from the characters in the trail.

The trail is deliberately obscure and involves puzzles that have themselves spawned sites and chat rooms dedicated to solving them; in particular http://www.for-evan.com/story.html. Visit that site and you will gain some idea of the mind-boggling complexity of the back story. It certainly absorbed the puzzle-solving audience. According to one of the for-evan group the e-mails being sent into the group were arriving at the rate of some 25 e-mails every 40 minutes. The media momentum has also extended into offline reports in newspapers and on national television as the story has grown. Most satisfying for the trail followers, however, is probably the fact that the most successful of the solution sites have now found themselves being written into the story, as references to their existence have been inserted by Dreamworks into Jeanine Salla's site.

At the time of writing the film's receipts were not available and so calculating a return on the campaign was not possible, but there is no doubt that the complexity of the campaign, along with its skillful exploitation of the Web, means that we will see further back story campaigns created around other media events in the future.

KEY INSIGHTS

Giving all due credit to the creativeness of the campaign, the key to it from a marketer's point of view is its reliance on the community element of the Web. From a very small beginning (simply an unfamiliar job title inserted into a credit sequence) the campaign anticipates that enough people will turn to a specific search engine and see what comes up. From there the game, as Sherlock Holmes would say, is afoot. Because each individual is confronted by challenging puzzles they respond by doing exactly what made the Web in the first place – they form ad hoc communities of shared interest, in this case to solve the mystery. That in turn means that interest is rapidly multiplied and the campaign gains a momentum that eventually leads it to burst out onto national television news, giving enormous publicity without a moment's airtime being bought.

Key to that success is the fact that the online puzzle trail remains faithful to its own internal logic - it is of course a marketing tool for a film, but not only are there no overt plugs, there are quite simply no references to the film at all.

PEPSI AND YAHOO! COMBINE ONLINE/OFFLINE

Even such tried and trusted tactics as coupons and product point collection can be given new life from an injection of e-marketing. Pepsi, for example, has a Pepsi Stuff promotion, first run in 1996, in which points are printed onto its packaging for people to collect and redeem against branded goods. In 2000, however, under the influence of John Vail, Pepsi's new media and digital marketing director, the soft drinks company tried adding a new angle to the scheme. This time they opted to partner with the leading portal, Yahoo!

The way it worked was that Pepsi Stuff points were printed as a code onto Pepsi and Mountain Dew bottles. Customers went to the PepsiStuff.com site, registered, and typed in that code to find out how many points it equated. The points could then be redeemed for goods in the usual way, or else used to get discounts on a further range of goods at Yahoo! Shopping. There was a further digital twist in that those who wanted to could use their points for instant rewards such as song or screensaver downloads.

In a nice touch the drinks maker was careful not to exclude those without easy access to the Net at home or at school. A tie-up with Kinko's copy centers meant that customers could turn up at their nearest Kinko's with their bottle tops and exchange them for five free minutes of online access – long enough to access the Pepsi Stuff site and register their points.

As well as the online campaign Pepsi used radio and TV ads to promote the campaign, but managed to recoup some of the costs in savings on full color brochures. Where previously it had been necessary to print brochures for Pepsi Stuff goods they could now simply be shown on the Web. Furthermore all the usual costs of coupons and data collection were either done away with or passed on to partner Yahoo! For Yahoo! by return, the promotion represented a chance to recruit a new generation of points-wielding consumers who could partake in the portal's auctions using a mixture of Pepsi and more conventional currency.

A co-branded Website, http://pepsi.my.yahoo.com/ was set up as a personal portal. By entering their details consumers can set up their own home page to display the news or horoscopes of their choosing. Unsurprisingly it leads heavily with music, and in a further neat piece of brand tie-in it currently features Britney Spears who just happens to be in the latest Pepsi ad (available on the site).

In its first eight weeks the Pepsi Stuff site harvested over two million registered users, and of course as with any promotion that involves real world goods being sent to postal addresses it could be sure that it had only genuine names and addresses. Pepsi regard that database as an invaluable building block for further marketing campaigns. So successful was it that the site remains online, and Pepsi has promised to run the promotion again in autumn 2001.

Most important of all was the image factor. Pepsi's Vail noted at the time that the company's consumer base were "walking away from their television sets" and "clicking online" instead. Research suggests that he is right in that children in homes with Internet access tend to spend fewer hours in front of the television, so reaching them means getting more of the Pepsi message online. From a branding point of view, the "next generation" message ties in with the image of the Web, and the choice of Yahoo! as a partner was also in line with the young and vivacious image of the product.

KEY INSIGHTS

Pepsi's success was based on two key points. The first was the recognition that online promotion could make an already successful conventional campaign even more successful both in terms of brand message, and the quality of response.

The second was in opting to proceed by means of a partnership, a symbiotic relationship with an existing online brand, rather than trying to reinvent the wheel and forge a major online presence all by itself. It's also worth noting that the company found a neat way of getting around the problem of including all those customers who don't have online access.

GAME AND VIDEO VIRAL MARKETING

Sooner or later everyone with an e-mail address has received a list of jokes, sometimes from a good friend, sometimes because they happened to be on a hijacked mailing list. The good jokes, the ones that made people laugh out loud, were almost always then forwarded on to other friends, colleagues, and family members. That fast-spreading viral approach has been eyed enviously by e-marketers around the globe looking to build awareness campaigns, including such disparate examples as Honda in the US, Johnny Walker Whisky in Germany and Heinz in the UK.

Honda's campaign featured short films of ordinary enough scenes with amusing things going on in them. In one example, a boat made of chairs rows through an office scene; in another a man in protective clothing clears a beach with a biohazard warning prior to stripping off himself and enjoying the sunshine. They raise a smile, and because they were specifically created to be less than one megabyte in size they are easy to send on. That size was also chosen specifically because the agency responsible, The Leith Agency, found that many office "firewalls" (software that protects computer networks) would block anything bigger.

The video has the necessary "look at this" factor while opting to avoid heavy branding in favour of discreetly mentioning a URL for a site which promotes the Honda Civic. The whole idea was to subtly play on the perception of the Honda Civic as sensible and for the middle-aged by adding an element of fun and youthfulness (inherent in the medium). If people want to see more of the films all they have to do is visit the Honda Civic site where there is a selection of them, plus the opportunity to register to receive the next series.

Some viral classics seem slightly less intentional. The Website Adcritic.com features short video clips of ads from around the world, and when the John West Salmon ad was featured on the front page it promptly became a cult classic in its own right, and was rapidly forwarded around the Internet. An image of a fisherman battling a bear for a salmon initially looks realistic, if bizarre, until the bear starts dropping into roundhouse kicks and a series of uppercuts. Again the intention of the campaign was to give a younger feel to a product not previously seen as youthful, and the spread of the ad on the Net, well in advance of most British people seeing it on TV helped add to the appeal. According to one report the ball was set rolling simply by an executive at agency Leo Burnett mailing it out to friends and family.

Games too can have that viral factor, sometimes to an unexpected degree. In Germany Johnny Walker branded a downloadable game about grouse shooting called Moorhuhn. The fact that Johnny Walker faces a brand rival called Famous Grouse brings another tongue-in-cheek dimension to the game, but otherwise there is nothing unusual in a brand's logo popping up in gaming – Chupa Chups sweets were doing so years ago. Except that this time *Media Matrix* reports that 20% of all the 8.9 million German households with online access visited the site (www.moorhuhn.de), in the process beating the record set by the German version of "reality TV" program Big Brother.

KEY INSIGHTS

The key to all of these examples is that if something is funny or entertaining enough the medium will reproduce it and pass it on as fast as a marketer could wish. It's crucial, however, to note that in each of these cases the amount of branding was kept to a minimum. In the Johnny Walker game the Walker logo is only there in the opening screen; in the John West video the name only pops up at the end; and throughout the now extensive Honda Civic campaign the videos end with a URL for a Honda site, nothing more.

The evidence seems to suggest that the best campaigns play down the extent to which they are a marketing ploy, and lean more heavily on humor than on branding. In the process they obtain a reach and impact that more heavy-handed techniques would not.

ONLINE BRANDING WITH BANNERS BY BRITISH AIRWAYS

As clickthrough rates have declined so the emphasis on the banner ad as a means of driving traffic has lessened, and a number of marketers have mounted campaigns that work more as a branding exercise than an invitation to click.

British Airways was looking for ways of raising awareness of its luxury facilities, and in particular the innovative offering of a truly flat bed in business class. At the time (autumn 2000) however, flat bed equipped planes were only available on flights out of JFK airport, and so the company experimented with a campaign aimed at a relatively local branding. A micro site (separate from the main British Airways home site) was created, and increased traffic to it was seen as a plus but definitely a secondary goal.

US new media specialists I-traffic (part of Agency.com) created a campaign featuring banner ads which were animated to show a glass of wine or a cup of coffee being poured – but seen from the perspective of someone lying down. The horizontal format of the banner lends itself nicely to that concept and while the words "click to see the bed" appeared on the banner it made its point about the product without the user having to respond at all. As a humorous touch some ads allowed users to click on banners to hear "bedtime stories" about the three bears.

The ads were placed on likely financial titles, and the backroom tracking technology set up to pay particular emphasis to where customers came from (some dial-up access accounts give clues as to where they come from); and of course there was a registration procedure which enabled the marketers to spot which interested customers were likely to benefit from the JFK flights.

Interestingly, although clickthrough was not intended to be the goal, the rate as reported by Channel Seven (www.channelseven.com) was 41% – considerably higher than average.

British Airways claimed that the geo-targeting was highly efficient, and that the advertisement delivery system was able to identify and correctly target a high number of people who lived in the target area. Certainly the company says it intends to do the same again as they roll out the flat beds on flights operating from other airports.

KEY INSIGHT

The main point about the British Airways campaign is that a little lateral thinking took them away from the traditional traffic driving model and into branding and geo-targeting. The fact that they did achieve better than average clickthroughs in the process came as an unexpected plus.

A study at the end of 2000 by AdRelevance, a Jupiter Media Matrix company, showed that ads building awareness accounted for 63% of online ads. Online is fast becoming an awareness forum, rather than the hard sell location it looked like when populated entirely by computer manufacturers trying to sell kit at low margins.

It should also be noted from the British Airways example that the ability to geo-locate makes it possible to avoid raising expectations in a customer base that is not going to benefit from a new service.

USING E-MAIL MARKETING TO CONVERT BROWSERS INTO SHOPPERS

The majority of customers put items into their online shopping trolley, but then leave the site without completing the transaction. In some cases this is simply down to site design – they find they can't get a total price including tax and shipping until they actually arrive at the "till." But with surveys suggesting that as many as eight out of ten customers abandon the goods in their online trolleys, many retailers have felt there is a major opportunity to convert some of those walk-outs into sales.

Reflect.com is a US beauty products site that specializes in allowing online customization of products. That in itself is an apt use of the medium, since it encourages the user to interact in more depth with the site.

The process begins with a beauty consultation in which a series of questions (developed with dermatologists and beauticians) allows the site to identify user needs. Based on the information received the site develops custom formulations of products, and then caps it all by allowing the user to select the product's fragrance, packaging, and even name. All in all it's a great USP (unique selling proposition) and one that allows for a lot of dialogue with the customer. Which makes it all the more regrettable when those customers leave without completing transactions.

So in conjunction with e-marketers Digital Impact, Reflect.com started to target the walk-outs with e-mail designed to help bring them back to the site, overcome their reservations about online shopping, and encourage both that sale and future loyalty. This involved a trial of different messages. The simplest noted that the customer had nearly but not quite purchased, and gave reassurances about the safety of online payment, the money-back guarantee, and different payment options (many customers still hesitate to give out credit card details online). To help turn them back the mail also offered a free lipstick (customized, naturally) if they went back and completed the order.

The next trial message was more specific in that it identified the exact object that was put in the trolley but not bought. As well as the assurances contained in the first e-mail, this one offered to give that particular item to the customer free, if they bought another customized item on their return – the idea being that the incentive would be greater with a free item in which the customer had already expressed interest.

The third e-mail test went a stage further. It looked out for users who picked up but then put back a bottle of shampoo. This email not only identified the shampoo, but included a picture of it with the customer's name on the label, thereby reinforcing the marketing message of customization. In this case the free gift offered as an incentive was complementary to the shampoo that had attracted the attention – in this case a conditioner.

Perhaps unsurprisingly, conversion rates for the second e-mail were better than those of the first, and conversion rates of the picture e-mail were more than double those of the simple reminder note.

KEY INSIGHTS

The case of Reflect.com is a great example of a site using e-mail to strengthen the dialogue it has with its customer, an engagement that also, rather neatly, helps reinforce the branding of the site.

What the e-mail results show are that with each further step of interaction the reward was greater, so that a simple reminder mail and promotional offer only went so far. To go the extra mile the campaign noted exactly what caught a shopper's eye, and then reinforced that with a promotion tailored to that need. The fact that the technology could do that without expensive and time-consuming human intervention highlights one of the strengths of e-commerce. E-mail marketers and online shops of all kinds would do well to take note of Reflect.com's campaign.

Key Concepts and Thinkers

A guide to major related influences upon e-marketing:

» affiliate marketing;
» adaptive marketing;
» banner ads;
» *Cluetrain Manifesto*;
» CRM;
» database marketing;
» e-customer;
» one-to-one marketing;
» permission marketing;
» relationship marketing;
» viral marketing;
» *The Tipping Point*; and
» influentials.

AFFILIATE MARKETING

This term refers to the system by which affiliate companies, as represented by their Websites, are allowed commission for referring customers to the principal site, based on what those customers then spend.

ADAPTIVE MARKETING

This is a part of McKenna's "relationship marketing" (see below). It involves being prepared to adapt the product or service itself, depending on the needs or reactions of the target market. That means less emphasis on deluging a market with a chosen message, and more flexibility in terms of communicating and providing "back channels" whereby customer feedback can return to the marketer and be acted upon.

BANNER ADS

The format pioneered in 1994 by Hotmail, a banner is a set size of advertisement that simply appears on the top of the Website and encourages the user to click on it, an action which then transports that user to the advertiser's site.

Banner ads evolved to include animation, even limited video, and became known as *Rich Media* banners. Some of these can now support transactions within the banner so that the user never leaves the host site.

The banner also evolved into the *tower ad* (which runs down the side of the screen); spawned the *pop-up* (a separate ad window that pops up within the user's browser); and bred the *interstitial* (a message that appears while a selected page is still loading up onscreen). For the first few years of the Web they were the essential building blocks of advertising before clickthrough rates (the percentage of people who clicked on them) declined.

THE *CLUE TRAIN MANIFESTO*: "THE END OF BUSINESS AS USUAL"

For some, the *ClueTrain Manifesto* is the pinnacle of modern marketing thinking. For others, it is insufferably pretentious (it is modeled on

Martin Luther's challenge to the Catholic church); not to mention a rambling collection of marketing opinions.

There were originally 95 different "theses" posted on the Website, not all of which seemed to deserve the same attention – one is simply a line from an Elvis song. However the initial, and most famous, thesis is that "markets are conversations" and that the Web now means that consumers are realizing that "they get far better information and support from one another than from vendors."

Championed by *Fast Company* magazine and described as "the future of business" by the *Wall Street Journal*, the *ClueTrain Manifesto* turned into a book of the same name, consisting of elaborations on the theme by the four collaborators (Rick Levine, Christopher Locke, Doc Searle, and David Weinberger).

On the way the *ClueTrain Manifesto* also takes a swingeing and entirely justified sideswipe at the artificial corporate voice so often employed in marketing. A counterbalance to more conventional views of corporate communications, its response to the traditional militaristic marketing language of "targets," "bombarding people with messages," "launches," and "campaigns" is to invite traditional business to the party: "put on this Hawaiian shirt, grab some chips and dip, and join in. But first you gotta loosen your grip on that assault weapon." Frank to the last, the *ClueTrain Manifesto* concludes with the assurance that "no, at the end of all this we don't have a cogent set of recommendations."

CRM (CUSTOMER RELATIONSHIP MANAGEMENT)

In the book *Loyalty.com* (McGraw Hill, 2000) Fredrick Newell defines CRM as "a process of modifying customer behavior over time, and learning from every interaction, customizing customer treatment and strengthening the bond between the customer and the company." In short, efficient data capture about customer behavior and appropriate response to customer feedback. As such, CRM is closely related to, and arguably a key part of such approaches as adaptive and permission marketing.

Once recognized as one of the hot topics of recent years CRM as a term has largely been taken over by technologists vying with each other to automate the process so that companies can manage customer relationships, even in mass markets. The desire to automate has led to some cynicism over the issue. Some companies are promoting automatic e-mail replies as CRM; others see this less as relationship management and more as computerized fobbing off.

One of the practical areas where CRM is being shouted loud and clear is that of unified messaging. The idea is that when you phone a call center to complain about a service or ask for details, the screen in front of the call center worker should also pop up the information that you have already e-mailed twice, faxed a note, and written a letter. CRM tracking systems within companies work so that even a single customer e-mail can be traced to see to whom it was routed, and what action they took over it.

The potential there for one-to-one marketing is vast – the reality, sadly, is that the companies that have implemented this kind of system are lamentably few and far between. In *Loyalty.com* Newell argues that most companies attempting to create customer loyalty are going about it all wrong. Worse, those with the most aggressive "loyalty programs" have the least loyal customers. Newell's argument is that software can be designed to predict what a customer will want before they even know they want it, and that a smart company can step in at that point and address that precise customer to suggest that particular product.

DATABASE MARKETING

This is based upon the use of computers to collect data which can then be analyzed to build up a picture of the consumer, enabling the vendor to market more effectively. Or as Seth Godin puts it in *Permission Marketing*: "Direct marketers are responding to this glut [of marketing information] by using computers. With access to vast amounts of computerized customer information, marketers can collate and cross-reference a database of names to create a finely-tuned mailing list, and then send them highly targeted messages. For example, a direct marketer might discover that based on past results, the best prospects for its next campaign are single women who are registered Democrats, who make more than $58,000 a year, and have no balance on their credit card. This information is easily available, and marketers are now racing to make their direct marketing ever more targeted."

THE E-CUSTOMER

"Technology is changing faster than customers, customers are changing faster than organizations, and organizations are changing faster than the people who run them. Catch up. In a world of 6.5 million different dot.com domains and millions more channels, the e-customer will never run out of places to be rather than being with you."

Max Mckeown, E-Customer (FT Books, 2000)

Max Mckeown started his e-customer apprenticeship with First Direct (telephone banking pioneers), developed leading edge e-solutions with software house AIT, and is currently strategic advisor for a number of global e-business ventures. Most famous for his championing of the e-customer he laid down the ground rules for dealing with this ever-growing force of commerce in his book *E-Customer*: "He just got smarter and faster, catch up."

Mckeown points out that "Perhaps the dissatisfied e-customer knows something you don't" and stresses the importance of dialogue: "Invitations to the e-customer to give you ideas for improvements or to share complaints are not meant to be textual padding. Such initiatives increase expectations and so demand serious, rigorous management." In the process he believes that the business model itself will have to evolve. "You need to blur the boundaries of business by providing valuable services without receiving direct payment. Such services are not expensive or difficult to establish but they give the e-customer a stake in what you are doing. You become his agent. Part of the same team. And that can become very powerful. The product needs to mean something in the real world and in the real psyche of the e-customer. That is the true nature of e-customer loyalty."

Which is where Mckeown meets CRM.

ONE-TO-ONE MARKETING

With the *One-to-One Future* (Doubleday, 1993) Don Peppers and Martha Rogers emphasized that often-cited yet rarely exploited piece of wisdom that it costs considerably more to acquire a new customer than it does to retain a current one.

Peppers and Rogers demonstrated that a company experiencing a customer churn rate of 25% per annum could add 100% to their bottom line simply by reducing that churn to 20%. In order to achieve this they proposed the idea of shifting mindset from the familiar approach of market share and turning instead to the idea of customer share – the amount of revenue from each individual customer. That in turn required a re-focusing on the individual, or as the authors put it: "In the one-to-one future it won't be how much you know about all of your customers that's important, but how much you know about each of your customers."

Peppers and Rogers took that a step further in 1997 with the publication of *One-to-One Enterprise*. By 1997 the impact of the Web was becoming clear, and with it the potential for tracking customers, enabling interactive dialogue and "mass customization".

One-to-one marketing is very much akin to McKenna's relationship marketing in approach but, being a product of the Web era it is able to put more detailed emphasis on what are recognizable as the keystones of online marketing. In particular it stresses the need for convenience and incentives when encouraging customers to interact, as well as establishing trust in the relationship. Peppers and Rogers were ahead of the game in recognizing that one of the keys to this involved creating and displaying a binding privacy policy.

PERMISSION MARKETING

Taking up where Peppers and Rogers left off, Seth Godin's eponymous book lays down the thinking that true one-to-one marketing and permission marketing are a synergy encouraged by the Internet. The argument is that the Net provides the perfect mechanism for frequent and virtually free interaction between marketer and consumer, so allowing for ever more detailed information flow, and a relationship of trust by which that flow is maintained. As Godin puts it:

"Permission marketing is the cousin of one-to-one marketing. Where Peppers and Rogers begin the process with the first sale, permission begins the process with the very first contact.

"Permission marketing works to turn strangers into friends and then friends into customers. One-to-one marketing uses the very same techniques, incorporating knowledge, frequency, and relevance, to turn customers into supercustomers. One-to-one doesn't compete with permission marketing. It's part of the very same continuum. The one-to-one marketer takes the permission that's been granted after someone becomes a customer and uses that permission to create even better customers. The better the permission, the more profit created. The one-to-one marketer works to change his focus from finding as many new customers as he can to extracting the maximum value from each customer. The permission marketer works to change his focus from finding as many prospects as he can to converting the largest number of prospects into customers. And then he leverages the permission on an ongoing basis."

Seth Godin, Permission Marketing

Permission marketing also defines itself by contrast with interruption marketing – the standard approach of TV, radio, and print in which our program or reading is interrupted by an ad that tries to claim our attention. In light-hearted vein Godin defines the two techniques as if they were suitors looking for brides:

"THE TWO WAYS TO GET MARRIED"
"The Interruption Marketer buys an extremely expensive suit. New shoes. Fashionable accessories. Then, working with the best databases and marketing strategists, selects the demographically ideal singles bar."

"Walking into the singles bar, the Interruption Marketer marches up to the nearest person and proposes marriage. If turned down, the Marketer repeats this process on every person in the bar."

"If the Marketer comes up empty-handed after spending the entire evening proposing, it is obvious that the blame should be placed on the suit and the shoes. The tailor is fired. The strategy expert who picked the bar is fired."

"And the Interruption Marketer tries again at a different singles bar."

"If this sounds familiar, it should. It's the way most large marketers look at the world. They hire an agency. They build fancy ads. They 'research' the ideal place to run the ads. They interrupt people and hope that one in a hundred will go ahead and buy something. And then, when they fail, they fire their agency!"

"The other way to get married is a lot more fun, a lot more rational, and a lot more successful. It's called dating. A Permission Marketer goes on a date. If it goes well, the two of them go on another date. And then another. Until, after ten or twelve dates, both sides can really communicate with each other about their needs and desires. After twenty dates, they meet each other's families. And finally, after three or four months of dating, the Permission Marketer proposes marriage."

"Permission Marketing is just like dating. It turns strangers into friends and friends into lifetime customers. Many of the rules of dating apply, and so do many of the benefits."

RELATIONSHIP MARKETING

Regis McKenna wrote what is seen as the definitive guide to this technique with *Relationship Marketing* (Addison Wesley, 1991). The basic idea is that while mass production and mass marketing offer the compelling arguments of economy of scale, they leave plenty of scope for carving out market niches by creating products that more closely fit the needs of specific groups of customers.

In order to achieve such goals the vendors of products or services have to move away from a *prescriptive* model whereby marketing is all about telling the public why they need the product or service. Instead, relationship marketing is about making the move to a *dialogue* with customers, and being prepared to re-think and if necessary re-invent product offerings depending on their feedback. Although McKenna's *Relationship Marketing* precedes the *ClueTrain Manifesto* (and indeed the Web itself) it can be seen as a key step towards the *ClueTrain*'s principal argument that "markets are conversations".

The key point of *Relationship Marketing* is that good marketing is knowledge-based; in order to "own" a segment of the market an efficient marketing organization uses the company's own knowledge of products/channels/markets to identify target segments, and integrates the customer as closely as possible into the design process to ensure that there is as total a match as possible between company design and consumer need.

For the e-marketer of today it is probably McKenna's insistence on adaptive marketing that is most relevant. The advent of the Web adds a whole new dimension to adaptive marketing's emphasis on opening communications channels to customers and the use of feedback analysis to convert information into intelligence.

VIRAL MARKETING

Steven Jurvetson, of Draper Fisher Jurvetson, the venture capitalists that funded Hotmail, is credited with coining the phrase "viral marketing" to describe the process whereby product information is spread by the electronic equivalent of word of mouth. By wrapping marketing messages in games, customer bonuses, or simply the "have you seen. . ." factor, consumers are themselves converted to marketers. Customers enlist friends and family as they try and solve puzzles or play games, or simply mail the offer on to acquaintances because there is a perceived benefit in recruiting them.

If skillfully managed, that marketing force can grow exponentially thanks to the speed and scope of modern communications, hence the comparison to a computer virus. Managed badly or intrusively however, and consumers can decide that a viral campaign is actually no more desirable than a real virus.

THE TIPPING POINT

Not specifically about marketing, although clearly relevant, *The Tipping Point* is a book (published by Little Brown) which examines what determines the point at which an idea, disease, or quirk, gains sufficient momentum to become a movement, an epidemic, or a fashion.

On the way, *The Tipping Point* considers the roles of key influencers ("mavens," or what Seth Godin calls "sneezers") who have the power to influence such turning points.

INFLUENCERS ON THE NET

A study by communications consulting firm Burson-Marsteller has tried to identify these individuals, whom it chooses to call e-fluentials.

According to Burson-Marsteller's CEO Christopher Komisarjevsky, these e-fluentials "have exponential power on the Internet. In the old economy – or the offline world – one person was generally thought to have an impact on the attitudes and behavior of approximately two people; however in the new economy, one influential online person has an impact on the attitudes and behavior of approximately eight people. The challenge today and in the future will be for companies, communities, and government agencies to understand e-fluentials and harness their potential impact to achieve measurable business results in this new e-society.''

The study further broke down the e-fluentials group into subspecies, defined as follows:

» Marketing Multipliers. These are the gurus of the new economy and e-markets, with opinions that are consequently extremely far-reaching because they tend to be propagated by the Web itself. Thus people like Seth Godin introduce major ideas but because they choose to make them available online they gain currency and reach at amazing speed.
» Influentials. These individuals are those whose sphere of influence extends beyond the Web and into the traditional business world, usually as a result of their jobs and positions.
» Avid Communicators. These communicate with more people online than the average, e-mailing widely and often.
» Information Sponges. Those who take pleasure in gleaning information by surfing the Web, and who then themselves become points of reference for others.
» Technology Savvy – the Internet experts. Of this group 74% go online more than once a day compared with 45% of the general online population; while 53% spend more than two hours a day online against 22% of the general online population.
» New Product Innovators. Those early adopters who buy first into new technologies and in doing so shape what works and what doesn't.

Burson-Marsteller has set up a Website that identifies whether or not a person is an e-fluential at http://www.efluentials.com/.

Resources

Where to find information, from such sources as:

» industry portals and community sites;
» publications;
» discussion groups;
» research companies;
» advertising organizations; and
» elsewhere.

INDUSTRY PORTALS AND COMMUNITY SITES

www.digitrends.net

The Information Network for Interactive Marketers is a gem in terms of gauging industry opinion. Wide swathes of e-marketing are covered, although the emphasis is more on comment and analysis than statistics. As such it is a lively industry forum and has very useful news and opinion sections dedicated to the two main areas; advertising/marketing and e-business.

http://www.i-advertising.com

Going back to 1996, I-Advertising claims to be the original community for Internet advertising and marketing professionals. It still provides industry information and news as well as educational and networking opportunities through the I-Advertising Discussion List and features useful directories of resources. Best of all it features an industry FAQ (as and when the community bulletin board is up and running) for interactive advertising which answers such useful questions as; "What's the average response rate for Internet advertising?" "What are the standard ad sizes and specs?" and "What's an insertion order?" Community members are invited to submit both questions and answers.

http://www.mediapost.com

Mediapost has been going since 1996, making it a rival to I-Advertising as one of the earliest advertising and media portals. It features free tools, news, and directories to help members plan and buy both traditional and online advertising, including The Media-Knowledge Base Directory, the *MPlanner* Web-based flowchart tool, an online system for buying ads on Websites (*immediabuy*) and the Center for Media Research. MediaPost also features a media magazine and industry seminars.

www.netimperative.com

Once the affirmed home page of any number of UK e-marketers, Net Imperative bucked the system recently by opting to switch to a paid service. Its promise is that it gives you an archive of over 10,000 articles, free and discounted events every month, and a PDA service at £50 for six months.

Primarily of interest to London-based marketers due to its free seminars, it continues to offer free news for those who aren't sure about subscribing, and invites newbies to come along to seminars gratis to find out about the company before signing up. NetImperative aims to expand its seminar base to other areas of the UK in the near future.

www.clickz.com

One of the most thorough sites for coverage of e-marketing, a glance at the pull-down menu of different topics shows that it has intelligently subdivided the many issues into their own categories either by technology or marketing approach. If you want research specifically on B2B or recent e-mail campaigns, this is a useful starting point not least since a weekly column selects case studies from the world of e-mail marketing.

PUBLICATIONS

The Industry Standard

http://www.thestandard.com

Set up as the insider's guide to the online community by refugees from *Wired* magazine, the *Industry Standard* has become something of an industry bible covering the larger issues such as politics and lifestyle as well as technology and commerce. Probably best known for its stats section (in conveniently ready-to-use PowerPoint presentation slide form), it has a specific media and marketing channel at http://www.thestandard.com/section/0,1970,816,00.html

This is further broken down to focus on specific subjects such as CRM, direct marketing, or affiliate marketing. Not a marketing specialist per se but good for news and analysis of its effect on online business.

Revolution Magazine

www.revolutionmagazine.com

Revolution is unusual in that it has three print editions and three corresponding sites covering the UK, US, and Asia as well as daily e-mail newsletters. The Asian coverage is not as complete as the US, but what there is can be sufficiently eye-opening about the difference between Asian and Western use of media, particularly in the use of mobile phones.

While it is ostensibly about the new economy in general the real strength of the magazine is its new media marketing expertise. Unlike many other weeklies, *Revolution*'s articles tend to be lengthy and in depth, including a large number of case studies, rather than the columns and industry commentary approach favored by the likes of *Digitrends*.

Advertising Age

www.adage.com

The Website of *Advertising Age* magazine and archive of articles relates to both interactive and conventional advertising and marketing. The site does not attempt to be a comprehensive reflection of the full paper-based content of *Advertising Age*, but on the other hand the online archive represents pretty much all the content from the interactive version. If the "search" facility is a little hard to find (you won't see it on the home page), it's because you need to register before you can search the archives, but registration is short and simple, and there is no charge.

Advertising Age's interactive coverage at www.adage.com/interactive/index.html includes daily news on interactive advertising, e-mail newsletters, and the details of the Ad Age 100 top interactive agencies by revenue. It also features an international section, which goes someway towards compensating for the US bias of the majority of e-marketing titles.

Business 2.0

www.business20.com

Business 2.0 has had a bit of a roller coaster ride, having launched and then folded in Europe before selling its US arm to online giants AOL/Time Warner.

Business 2.0 caters for an audience of individuals it dubs "transformers" (Godin dubs them "sneezers") who are the key influencers of the so-called new economy. Although its focus is on the whole of e-commerce, Business 2.0 does have a separate marketing section at www.business20.com/marketing/index.htm.

Ad Week

www.adweek.com

Weekly magazine with online section on news and features of the advertising industry. Not exclusively dedicated to interactive advertising, but features a dedicated interactive section at http://www.adweek.com/adweek/iq_interactive/index.jsp

Fast Company

http://www.fastcompany.com/

Dubbing itself as the magazine for the new economy, *Fast Company* has undoubtedly been quick to see the trends coming; as for example with its championing of the *ClueTrain Manifesto*. It is not a specifically marketing-orientated title, however, and doesn't break down its material to separate out a marketing section, although the range of articles means that astute use of the search facility will often dig out answers to your questions.

DISCUSSION GROUPS

Online Advertising Discussion List

http://www.o-a.com

The Online Advertising Discussion List focuses on professional discussion of online advertising strategies, results, studies, tools, and media coverage. The list also provides editorial coverage of conferences of interest to people in the online advertising industry. Subscription is free.

UK Net Marketing

UKNM is the UK's leading discussion group for everything from favorite ad of the moment, to who are the best PR companies for online work, and where to find those elusive statistics. Informal and informative, it provides a useful reality check for gauging just what problems other e-marketers are having in the real world. To apply to join the lists go to the mail hub at http://www.chinwag.com/

RESEARCH COMPANIES

Forrester

http://www.forrester.com

With research by consumer section, technology, industry and region, Forrester is a useful source of market analysis. Indeed for some areas, particularly the impact of new media on old, and the spectacular growth of e-mail marketing, Forrester has become the definitive source. Specifically there is a section on digital marketing, although the number of full reports on offer was only two at time of writing. The site requires registration, but still pulls its punches since while overviews and précis are available, full reports are charged for.

eMarketer

www.emarketer.com

"We do the work – you get the credit" is the boast of eMarketer, with a site which pools information from over 350 of the industry publication and government reports to create the "eStat Database," usually within 24 hours of publication. This, says eMarketer, makes it the world's leading provider of Internet and e-business statistics. Reports combine original analysis with aggregated numbers from leading sources world-wide. Online newsletters are then created and e-mailed out to registered users.

Ipsos Reid

www.ipsosreid.com

Ipsos Reid doesn't boast the breadth of coverage you'd expect from better-known players, but more than makes up for that with such promising sounding reports as "Why aren't more people online?" and "Are you satisfied?" For subscribers Ipsos Reid publishes *World Monitor*, a quarterly report of global public opinion highlighting consumers' responses to behavioral, attitudinal, and value-oriented questions about the world they live in. *World Monitor*'s subject matter covers anything from materialism, to spiritualism, to sex.

Cyberatlas

http://cyberatlas.internet.com

This site has a superb "big picture" section looking at the demography and geography of Net use. Anyone hunting down numbers should start with the Cyberatlas "Stats Tool Box" which has an impressive array of figures. Archived data goes back to 1998, and the reports on e-business include detailed roundups of the top sites, e-tailers, consumer spending etc.

Cyberatlas also goes into the linguistics of the Web in some detail with breakdowns of how the languages are adding up online. If ever in doubt about the worldwide nature of the Web, Cyberatlas is the place to visit to put it all into perspective.

Global Reach

http://www.euromktg.com/globalstats

With much talk of "maximizing international revenue streams" Global Reach promises that the Internet "makes it possible to reach overseas markets as easily as if they were next door." A slight exaggeration but it's certainly a starting point for those charged with global ambitions.

The company promotes overseas (i.e. non US) Websites, and offers global sales strategies as well as having a selection of translation agencies, multilingual Websites, solutions for small and large companies, and consultancies etc. A clearing house of the internationally aspirant, but also a useful place simply for its at-a-glance stats, not only of what languages are online, but their percentage of the online population and a representation of them as a percentage of the world economy.

Jupiter Research

www.jup.com for signed-up subscribers

www.jmm.com for the marketing matrix – indices of performance and prediction.

Jupiter Research provides strategic analysis and insight on how the Internet and new technologies change the way companies do business; but the stock-in-trade for which Jupiter is valued are its industry predictions. If you want to know how much the US will spend on ITV advertising over the next four years, then Jupiter is the place to go.

Never afraid to put numbers on the most blue-sky technologies or trends, Jupiter has been the savior of many a marketer charged with producing a coherent-sounding presentation that looks well beyond the truly foreseeable future.

Iconocast

www.iconocast.com

Iconocast is a new media company that supplies facts, figures, trend analysis and insider information in the Internet marketing industry. It features weekly e-mail newsletters ("more concentrated than the leading brand"), a gossip columnist "The Jacobyte," and a new resource, "Prosumer.tv," aimed at the field of digital convergence.

ADVERTISING RESOURCES

@d:tech

www.ad-tech.com

Describing itself as the "World's Leading Event for Interactive Advertising, Marketing and Commerce," @d:tech offers case studies, research premieres and networking opportunities at its regular US industry summits.

Affiliate Marketing; Information on Affiliate Directories

http://adres.internet.com/business/affiliate/

includes details on Refer-it, AffiliateMatch.com, Associate-it.com, AssociatePrograms.com, Cashpile, and I-revenue.net.

Channel Seven, Turbo Ads, and Wireless Ad Watch

These sibling sites offer a broad view of the industry, broken down into a number of main areas:

» ChannelSeven.com – NewsBeat | Ad/Insight | Spotlight | Get It To Go
» TurboAds.com – Rich Media News | Case Studies | Broadband
» WirelessAdWatch.com – NewsWatch | Insight | Profiles

Channel Seven is a rich source of case studies and analysis; Wireless AdWatch is one of the few sites focusing entirely on the development of mobile marketing; and Turbo Ads is seen as the home of Rich Media advertising, the current bright hope for breathing new life into banner advertising.

Ad Resource
www.adresource.com

Ad Resource is broken down into five main areas; Advertising, Business, Marketing, Software and Tools. Under "Marketing" the e-marketer will find awards, media guides, news releases, market research, spam watch, traffic measurement, specialty search engines, and opt-in mailing lists.

Internet Advertising Bureau
www.iab.net

Here is the first global, not-for-profit association devoted exclusively to maximizing the use and effectiveness of advertising on the Internet. On this site you will find information on IAB events, research, news and membership. Check out what's new at the IAB.

Apart from anything else this is the place to find the Internet Ad Revenue reports, and codes of good practice including privacy guidelines.

Internet Advertising Resource Guide
www.admedia.org

This site features a number of sections including Academia, Legal, Big Move, Innovations, and Research. Not a lot of content in itself, but there are useful links out to sites for the major steps of a campaign – planning, development, management, and research.

Internet Advertising Reporter
www.internetnews.com/IAR

Internet News' Advertising Report features the latest news on US agencies and products as well as e-mail news alerts.

Web Marketing Today Info Center
www.wilsonweb.com/webmarket

Links to articles about effective Web marketing, and to online resources for business. From its beginning in August 1995, the Web Marketing Info Center has become one of the most comprehensive Web marketing sites of its kind on the Internet. Wilson Web promises to continue adding articles and resources to this site every month.

In particular this is a good starting point for the e-market newbie who is "overwhelmed and overloaded," and looking for basic checklist approaches to promoting Websites and attracting visitors.

OTHER RESOURCES

Clue Train Manifesto

www.ClueTrain.com

Now that the manifesto has been turned into a Perseus book, from which the authors presumably hope to make a profit, the original (and still free) *ClueTrain* site is a pale shadow of its former self, albeit still something of a tourist attraction for e-marketers.

The Big Red Fez

http://www.thebigredfez.com/

Home to fez-wearing monkeys everywhere, this is also the place to register for occasional e-mail newsletters from Seth Godin, Jim Sterne, and Target Marketing of Santa Barbara, www.targeting.com

Jim Sterne is one of the most influential writers on such seminal marketing topics as CRM and email marketing. You can find out more about him, and information on his books, including synopses, introductions, and sample chapters from such titles as:

» *World Wide Web Marketing*, 3rd Edition
» *Customer Service on the Internet*, 2nd Edition
» *What Makes People Click*, (Advertising on the Web)
» *E-mail Marketing*, (Build customer relationships)
» *E-Metrics*, 67-page white paper

Recommended reading

One-to-One Future by Don Peppers and Martha Rogers (Doubleday, 1993).

One-to-One Enterprise by Don Peppers and Martha Rogers (Doubleday, 1997)

Relationship Marketing by Regis McKenna (Addison Wesley, 1991).

Loyalty.com by Fredrick Newell (McGraw Hill, 2000).

One of the better-known explorations of the possibilities of CRM.

One-to-one Web Marketing by Cliff Allen, Deborah Kania, and Beth Yaeckel (John Wiley).

Now in its second edition, this book lays down the practical steps towards implementing a one-to-one approach to Web development and e-mail marketing.

CyberMarketing

Collection of essays on interactive marketing, edited by Edward Forrest, Regina Brady, and Richard Mizerski (NTC Business Books).

Ten Steps to Making E-Marketing Work

And here they are!

1. planning;
2. tie-in to offline;
3. internet presence;
4. promotion from the home page;
5. promotion off the home page;
6. online transactions;
7. recording, reporting, analysis;
8. listening;
9. talking; and
10. managing.

1. PLANNING

In the mid 1990s we saw what is now referred to as the first generation of commercial Websites. As URLs cropped up on hip TV ads and magazine pages it became a necessity to have a Website, and the first task of any e-marketer was usually to have one built. That was it – just having something with the "www" prefix was enough, never mind the fact that there was no real reason for anyone to go there. With a billion indexed pages already in existence it is now very hard for any new site to gain attention. Most don't; in fact, most have no real reason for their existence other than as an excuse for a client to have "www..."on their business card.

Successful e-marketing requires planning, and before planning on why a consumer should want to know more about you and your campaign there are some questions the e-marketer has to ask. Firstly, what is the point of the campaign? Is it simply to drive Web traffic to an existing site? This was the original aim of most banner advertising, and is still an important tool, but no longer the only one for the e-marketer.

A branding exercise, aimed at creating an image or association? This undoubtedly requires close attention to both form and function. It is surprising how many reputable product brands have blotted their e-copybooks by "cheap" tactics such as spamming.

An exercise in building awareness? If there is a particular message about a product function or benefit then the principles of relationship marketing will probably come into play.

Are you simply telling random individuals about something, or are you targeting a group and setting up a channel for their feedback to find out if your offering matches their interests?

A direct response or transaction campaign where the interactive medium encourages the consumer to react by buying or requesting something?

These questions are by no means mutually exclusive, but without clear goals the rest of the e-marketing exercise will be just that, merely an exercise.

2. TIE-IN TO OFFLINE

With a few exceptions online campaigns are just part of a company's marketing effort, yet despite that, multimedia, Web development, indeed all things technological, have historically been developed in isolation from the marketing department.

When planning a conventional marketing campaign few marketers would overlook the importance of integrating the different media, with TV, print, direct mail, and poster ads all performing different but complementary tasks. When it comes to e-marketing, however, all that so often goes out the window. Companies that would insist on massively expensive TV commercials, and go through the print quality of magazine ads with a magnifying glass, often palmed off the Website to whoever would take on the job without a thought to consistency or brand values. While that trend is fortunately dying out there is another problem in that those who do bring in e-marketing as part of their main campaign still often do so after deciding a TV or print approach which they simply expect the new media workers to translate.

By bringing the different strategies together right at the planning stage (see above) they can best be used to complement each other fully. TV ads could drive people to Websites where they engage with the company more closely in return for rewards or simple amusement.

In some cases strategic e-marketers have turned to the Web because their avenues on TV were blocked. US brewer Miller, for example, decided to sponsor the online coverage of the Super Bowl partly because arch-rival Budweiser perennially outbid them for the prime TV times.

Deciding how to make online campaigns fit in with traditional marketing is all part of a successful long term mix.

3. INTERNET PRESENCE

A few years ago Internet presence meant registering your domain and putting up a page. A lot of marketers then folded their arms and waited for the world to beat a path to their doorstep. In fact your own site may not even be necessary at all since it may prove better to partner with another site. Even very well-established brands have come together to co-brand sites (see Chapter 7, Pepsi/Yahoo!).

Where there is a home site, however, it is not a case of "build it, they will come." Driving traffic to the site is one of the e-marketer's key tasks and to do that it helps to think beyond the confines of the traditional banner ad. Banner ads have their role, even more so as rich media expands their potential, as do pop-ups and interstitials (although there is the danger of alienating the audience with these in-your-face approaches). There are other means of expanding awareness and driving traffic, however, including Web rings (likeminded or similar sites recommend each other), and affiliate marketing (where referring sites get a cut of any purchases made).

4. PROMOTION FROM THE HOME PAGE

Mi casa es su casa. In an ideal situation your marketing home page is so comfortable for your consumer that you having driven them there, they then choose to make it their default home page – the first port of call each time they surf the Web. That's the approach adopted with great success by Pepsi/Yahoo! (see Chapter 7).

The Website is at the heart of most e-marketing strategies, and yet so many sites still consist of nothing more than "brochureware," where a print brochure is translated to the Web as a few pictures and descriptive text. There has to be a reason for consumers to go to the Web, whether that be games, humor, or promotions.

If the site is there to provide information it should try to offer something that users cannot get from other media, such as store finders where the user enters a post/ZIP code and finds out where the nearest outlet is. If offering promotions in return for registration information, there are a couple of points to remember. A study by the Promotion Marketing Association in the US showed that over 80% of consumers were happy to give out their occupation, e-mail and home address if they thought the reward was right. Offering rewards that have to be sent by post also ensures accurate post/ZIP codes at registration. However 84% of the survey's respondents have abandoned promotions that required too much, notably home phone numbers and income levels.

5. PROMOTION OFF THE HOME PAGE – VIRAL AND EMAIL

One of the fastest growing areas of e-marketing is e-mail marketing, and hand in hand with that goes viral marketing. Viral doesn't necessarily mean e-mail – a branded game or screensaver that is quickly passed around the office is a great viral tool for creating awareness that never once uses mail. That said, when most e-marketers refer to viral they mean mail.

Forrester estimates that e-marketers will send more than 200 billion e-mail messages by 2004, and demand for e-mail marketing services (often from specialized e-mail marketing services) will create a $4.8 billion industry by 2003. Forrester also estimates that e-mails will equal the volume of traditional direct mail in the US by 2003, and that by 2004 the average US household will be receiving nine marketing e-mails per day. Clearly then, this will turn into a sea of words unless e-marketers remember that this is not about broadcasting to customers, but about establishing dialogues.

E-mail marketing must offer value in some form, be it promotions or service, and the activity will only realize its full potential if allied to a thorough measuring system that tracks the degree of interaction and interest, rather than just monitor variations in purchasing patterns.

One of the reasons for the success of specialized bureaus is that they are estimated to achieve purchase rates up to four times higher than marketers who keep their e-mail in house. E-marketers might thus do well to look into outsourcing their e-mail.

6. ONLINE TRANSACTIONS/INTERACTIONS

While sales per se might seem beyond the remit of the e-marketer, getting to that point is all part of the job. Having caught the consumers' attention and drawn them to the site they will be frustrated if they can't then buy online and in a secure environment (never, ever, invite anyone to submit credit card details in plain e-mail).

However, there is more to purchasing than just handing over a card. Many people prefer to use the phone to finalize a sale. Call-back buttons can be put on a site which allow a user to enter a number and a time, and request a call from a marketer. They may want input on the product itself, as tried by Levis, who allowed women to enter their measurements and have jeans tailored to measure. Or Nike allowing Web users to enter a message that would then be printed onto the shoes they ordered.

7. RECORDING, REPORTING, AND ANALYSIS

None of which is of any use if all this rich data is going unrecorded. The Web offers unparalleled ability to collect detailed data, be it cost per impression, cost per click, effective yield, click-paths through sites, and even the geographical location of users. The question is how are you going to collect it and then comprehend it?

The answer for many is by turning to the measuring companies, such as DoubleClick and NetGravity, who either offer the service or the software to measure traffic and customize or rotate banner ads accordingly. Some packages such as "Clickshare" by Newshare not only measure traffic but also include modules for user registration and transactions, neatly bringing sales and marketing together.

For those on a budget that precludes bringing in a measuring service there is still a lot to be learnt simply by using statistical analysis patterns, and the log files that are automatically generated by Web servers.

8. LISTENING

One of the most chilling products to see the light of day is a software package that automates e-mail replies with an "appropriate" response. It scans customer e-mails, and picks out key words or phrases which match up with a set of commonly encountered complaints or comments, and creates a suitable reply. Only a company that has completely missed the point of e-marketing would find it tempting to appear caring while actually carrying on with business as usual.

Customer feedback is the key to success, and that means ensuring that there are channels in place. If the company has a call center, is it Web enabled? Or is an individual going to be in charge of answering e-mail? If so, is that their job, or will the task be given to someone who already feels fully employed on something else?

Too often marketing campaigns busy themselves with the issue of what they want to say to their markets, and too little with ensuring that they hear what their market wants to say to them. Nor does listening simply mean setting up occasional focus groups. Structured response in the form of feedback boxes, registration details and questionnaires are great – but don't forget more free form response too. Any site, game, or e-mail campaign that doesn't have a "mail to" option, or individuals named as e-mail correspondents, is missing the most important trick.

Bear in mind too that different audiences may communicate in different ways. For example, if you're targeting a youth group do you have a mechanism for "hearing" them if they choose to respond by, say, SMS text messaging? Or Internet chat?

9. TALKING – DIALOGUE AND CRM

Having set up the channels for consumers to talk back to you, there is now the issue of how to sustain the conversation. Is there simply going to be one person (presumably you as the e-marketer) whose job it is to talk on behalf of an entire company? That is an approach grounded in the mentality of the days of mass media when manufacturers could control the message. It is increasingly undermined today by the fact that chat rooms and bulletin boards are populated not only by your potential customers, but also your existing ones, disgruntled ex-customers, and employees (past and present).

A company that insists upon only talking through an official mouthpiece will usually provoke even more non-official comment. An alternative approach is for your CRM policy to embrace the idea that the company too should speak like a community. It is possible to filter and route e-mail and voice mail so that it is directed to the most appropriate person (not always the marketer); most importantly it can be tracked to ensure that there are no bottlenecks in the organization, or "serial deleters" who simply bin consumer feedback.

If you're likely to generate a significant amount of feedback you should perhaps consider outsourcing to professional call centers specializing in integrated media (electronic, voice, etc.), in which case you have to ensure that these continue to function as a way of bringing you closer to the customer, not providing a barrier to hide behind.

10. MANAGING E-MARKETING INTERNALLY

No one said this would be easy, and one of the biggest problems that an e-marketer is likely to face is not the job of interfacing with the consumers on the Web, but the problems of dealing with attitudes and people within the company.

Leaving aside the boardroom battles over the need for e-marketing at all (because if you've got this far they are presumably behind you), the next biggest problem is everyone else. Expecting everyone in a company to reinvent themselves as a communicator is unrealistic. There are those who are naturally good at the job, and there are those whose job or title means that they should be in the front row of consumer conversations. Sadly these two are not always one and the same person.

Just as you have to provide a reason why customers should interact with you and your message, so you'll have to provide motivation for those inside the company to play their part. An office-wide memo is not motivation. Remembering the importance of monitoring to e-marketing, it may be useful to establish a means of tracking and rewarding customer interaction – as long as it can be done without taking on the air of Big Brother. Creating a culture of knowledge-sharing will help. At its simplest that could mean setting up and publishing FAQ lists to help individuals within the company deal with questions from without. As a step further, dependent on resources and available time, it could mean establishing knowledge maps of the company (usually held on a corporate intranet) that make it easier to find experts within an organization – or just see who has dealt with this kind of query before.

KEY INSIGHTS

» Planning takes on even more importance when dealing with complex and possibly unfamiliar media.
» It is not enough just to have a Website.
» Extending your message across the Web means more than buying banner ads in a few high profile spots.
» Partnerships, affiliations, and e-mail or viral campaigns should all be part of the e-marketing mix.
» Measuring and tracking are possible with a degree of sophistication unimaginable outside of the online world – ensure you use them to good effect.

» More than any other medium the electronic world revolves around the ability of the market to reply and communicate – not just with you, but with each other.
» Building listening and dialogue into the marking plan becomes essential.

All of this involves a major shift in culture and approach. Managing that within your own organization will prove as big a challenge as getting the audience on your side.

Frequently Asked Questions (FAQs)

Q1: Why should I bother with e-marketing?

A: Because apart from the opportunity it offers to understand your markets (and be understood by them), it is where your audience is. Take a look at the timeline in Chapter 3 – The Evolution of E-Marketing – to get some idea of the speed of its growth.

Q2: How is e-marketing different from conventional marketing?

A: Not in the technology, though that has often blinded marketers, but in the difference it makes to the relationship with the market. See Chapter 2 to learn more.

Q3: I already have an interactive marketing company working for us: isn't that enough?

A: One of the problems the industry has is a lack of integration between e-marketing and the more conventional arms. Opting for outside expertise can prove an excellent way of getting up to speed, but it doesn't necessarily bridge the cultural and understanding gaps that may interfere with campaign co-ordination (see Chapter 2). If the marketing department comes to understand the thinking behind e-marketing it puts in place the final piece that pulls together a company's marketing efforts.

Q4: Does that mean unlearning everything I've built up in a long and successful marketing career?

A: No, it means re-thinking a lot of how media and markets interact, but much of the theory that now dominates online marketing was already evolving with regard to conventional and direct marketing. Writers such as Peppers and Rogers, and Regis McKenna, got the ball rolling on this some time ago, and their more wired counterparts such as Seth Godin are simply taking up the baton. See Chapter 8 – Key Concepts and Thinkers.

Q5: Does the World Wide Web mean instant global expansion?

A: Yes, but only if you're not careful. Read Chapter 5 before planning that office in Tuvalu.

Q6: Isn't e-marketing just for multinational corporations?

A: Not at all. E-marketing is about blurring the boundaries between marketer and market. It's just as valid for a small company with a short e-mail list as it is for IBM, although the scale, of course, is rather different.

Q7: Where can I go to find out more about this?

A: Chapter 9, Resources, contains all the discussion groups, bulletin boards, portals, Websites, and newsletters you could hope for. Oh, and even a couple of genuine paper books.

Q8: Why do I need to consider e-marketing? I already have banner ads.

A: Banner ads initially relied on the premise that online media worked much like offline media. As the more complex picture emerges so do their limitations and with that an understanding that they function best as part of a mix. See Chapter 3 – The Evolution of E-marketing.

Q9: With interactive TV on its way, should I even bother with getting to grips with the Web?

A: The impact of interactive TV is likely to be enormous, but it is still likely to function in conjunction with the Web. Besides, leaving aside the technology, which will always be evolving, the principle of interaction is the same for both approaches. See Chapter 6 – The State of the Art.

Q10: If I read this title, will I become a fully-formed e-marketing guru?

A: Sadly no, but you'll know a lot more of the questions you need to ask if you want to become one.

Index